Auto Ac  Playbook

Step by Step Field Guide to Writing Auto Damage Estimates as an Independent Adjuster or Auto Damage Appraiser

by
Chris Stanley

Cover by Shane Mikus

Contents

3

Introduction

Writing auto damage estimates can unlock new careers, freeing lifestyles, and earning potential that many people dream of but few ever have the chance to achieve.

Before learning to work insurance claims, for my entire "adult" life, I worked as a regular employee at a Target store and later at a Walmart Distribution center. When my father-in-law presented me with the opportunity to shadow him to learn the insurance claims business, I nearly balked and walked away…

I had never changed my own oil, didn't know a thing about cars, and had no vision for the future. Thankfully, I decided to change my shift at work and learn how to be an auto damage appraiser. I didn't know what that meant, but after six months of training, my father in law turned me loose on my own insurance claims, and now 11 years later, I look back and marvel at the journey I have had.

I've traveled the country, worked with companies like State Farm, USAA, numerous hail repair companies, and amazing individuals at body shops. I've worked with IA (independent adjuster) Firms, and other adjusters who can be found all over, from Florida up to New York, over to Colorado and most places in between. Through the training and mentorship I received from my father-in-law, my life was given a breath of fresh air, and here eleven years later, I want to pass it on.

My mentor was a painter, body man, and then a body shop manager before becoming an IA. I still call him to this day, and although I won't give you his phone number, I want to give you what he taught me, plus what I've learned over the years in this business.

This book is designed to be your MANUAL for writing auto damage claims as an adjuster or auto damage appraiser. The guidelines and protocols I outline in this book should not be a prison for you, but rather this book serves as a baseline of knowledge given by a mentor. YOU are the adjuster and you ultimately make the final call in your specific scenario. Use the information here to help you make a more educated decision.

I've done my best to not only write my best practices, guidelines, suggestions, and processes, but I have also sought the advice of various people in the business, auto body specialists and professionals from all walks of the industry, to bring you widely accepted "best practices".

Carrier and IA Firm guidelines you receive will ALWAYS trump the advice given here, but when you find yourself staring at a car, assignment, or screen and are unsure of what to do, just know, you have a book built upon the experience of industry experts here to help you.

This book is NOT a replacement for training, but a primer for someone who is new or a quick refresher to help you in a pinch. When you feel you need to phone a friend, I hope you'll consider this book your go-to resource. If you can't find the answer in this book, I hope that you'll head over to the IA Path Community, tapping into the massive amount of resources and people that are there to help you on your journey.

If you desire to be an independent adjuster or auto damage appraiser, THIS ENTIRE BOOK IS FOR YOU!

To organize the information you need, I have broken the book into 3 primary sections, the Process, the Parts, and the Playbook.

Part 1: The Process
Here you will learn about the process of being an independent auto damage adjuster or appraiser. You will start at the very beginning, walk you through receiving your first assignment, and continue with you you through the entire claim, including how to handle supplements.

Part 2: The Parts
This is where you will get a breakdown of the major components of vehicles, their names, best practices, standard operations, and/or prices for each part. This will be a great reference when standing at the vehicle wondering what something is called or how to write notes about it.

Part 3: The Playbook
I know that you will face many situations that you will want to ask questions about, the playbook is designed to give you a fighting chance with common situations.

Here you will find portions of some chapters from previous parts of the book pulled out for quick reference, plus specific scenario chapters to make your claim estimating career easier.

This book does NOT cover how to get the first claim or how to get started in this industry. If you need help learning about how to get started as an independent adjuster or auto damage appraiser, you can check out my book the **Independent Adjuster's Playbook**.

If you are trying to get IA Firms to hire you and wondering how to get more work as an IA, I'd recommend you check out a book I co-wrote with Kagan Blackburn called the **Networking Adjuster's Playbook.**

Now, are you ready to learn how to estimate auto body damage? Are you ready to walk with confidence in your new career? Then let's dive into the Auto Adjuster's Playbook.

All forms, templates, and guides discussed in this book can be found and downloaded at **IAPath.com/auto-downloads/**

Part 1: The Process

In this section of the book, we are going to cover the process of handling an auto claim. As an auto damage appraiser or field adjuster the process begins by receiving the assignment and ends with handling a supplement.

Let's GO!

Get the Guides!

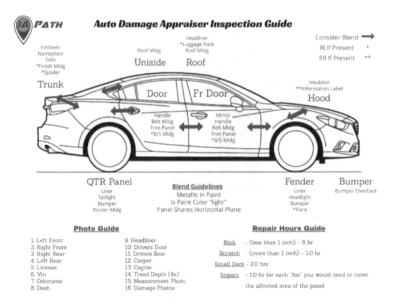

I will be referencing various guides I've created throughout this book.

You can get your free copy of all guides and forms listed in this book by heading to AutoAdjustersPlaybook.com/guides/

Receive the Assignment

Your stomach drops, and you break into a cold sweat...

You've received your first assignment!

Congratulations. If you haven't experienced the rush of getting your first assignment yet, trust me it's exhilarating.

IA Path Crash Star, (our affectionate term for our students who graduate from IA Path's Collision Course) Robert Nodine, said it best. After he received his first few claims from an IA Firm, "Just had another claim added. I feel like I've arrived, Chris!"

YES! That is how it feels until you realize you have no idea what to do... Fear not! I'm here to guide and remind you of the proper process and how to thrive as an Independent Adjuster/Appraiser (IA).

Step 1: Review the Assignment

Reviewing the assignment sheet is the very first step that must be taken when a new assignment is received. This first part of the process is very straightforward but important! There was one instance where I failed to review the assignment sheet and missed special instructions that were of the utmost importance…

I called the owner of the vehicle and ended up talking with a distraught wife… when I reviewed the assignment sheet it stated,

"Please do not contact the owner. Husband passed away in the accident. Contact the tow yard listed below."

Talk about feeling like a lazy jerk. That incident cemented in my mind the importance of reviewing the assignment sheet and guidelines.

When you review the assignment, you are going to look for a few specific things:

1. That the assignment is in your area (double check the vehicle location and special instructions)

2. Look for special guidelines or instructions

3. Verify the vehicle is within your skill set to handle (is it an RV, heavy equipment, or motorcycle?)

The Assignment Sheet

The example assignment sheet below replicates what appraisal and insurance company's assignment sheets look like. I'll go through each section to make sure you understand what you are looking at.

When an appraisal company assigns you an assignment (gives you work), they will email you an assignment sheet or a notification that this claim has been assigned to you. Whether in your email or in their online portal, the assignment sheet is where all the information the insurance company has placed all the information for this claim.

IA Path Example Assignment Sheet

File Number - 12021

Insurance Company – Stanley Insured

Date of Loss – 11/12/16

Type of Loss - Collision

Deductible - $500.00

Claim # - 00016789

Owner – Tango Zulu

Address – 15954 Jackson Creek Parkway, Monument Co 80132

Phone – 123-456-7890

Vehicle – 98 Dodge Ram B1500

VIN - 2B6HB11Y3WK137016

License Plate – 123-XYZ

Color – Gray

Damage Notes – Point of impact: Front Bumper, Insured rear-ended claimant vehicle

Special Instructions – Verify damage to the front of the bumper and look for paint transfer.

Client Guidelines

A/M Parts – Yes after 12 months

LKQ Parts – Whenever Possible

Release Estimate? – No

Total Loss – Provide a CCC Valuation Report, do not call in.

Now we'll review what all this information means and why it may be important.

File Number - This is the number that is associated with the appraisal company's file. I encourage you to have a file number associated with your claims (also could double as an invoice number). This number is only useful when speaking with the appraisal company that assigned it to you.

Insurance Company –This is the insurance company that initiated the assignment for an inspection. They are the ones paying for the inspection. The owner of the vehicle will likely not know the name of the appraisal company that assigned you the file, but they are familiar with the insurance company name. Ultimately, this is who is paying the bill for this inspection.

Date of Loss – This is the date that the claim incident took place on. Is important for you to be able to understand how long this claim has been ongoing before you call the owner. If the date of loss is more than a week old, it's possible this owner is getting impatient.

Type of Loss - The type of loss is referencing the type of coverage that the claim is falling under. IT DOES NOT MEAN THAT THE INSURANCE COMPANY HAS AGREED TO PAY UNDER THAT COVERAGE.

There are three common types of losses.

Collision - The insured of an insurance company has collision or "full coverage". If you see a collision type of loss, you can bet that the owner is the insured of the insurance company.

Liability - This is when an insurance company's insured has hit another vehicle. If you see liability, you are likely looking at a vehicle of an owner that is not insured with the insurance company and is the claimant.

Comprehensive – This is damaged caused by an act of God or an act of nature. Deer hits, hail damage, or squirrels chewing through wires classify as comprehensive losses.

Deductible - Very frequently misunderstood by most everyone, the deductible is simply the amount the insurance company "deducts" before paying out on a claim.

If an owner has a $500 deductible and has a $1000 claim, the insurance company will issue a check for $500. The owner is not required to pay that up front to file the claim, but the owner is required to pay it to a repair facility after the conclusion of the repairs. If repairs never take place, the owner is never required to pay anything. The insurance company picks up the tab after the deductible has been paid by the owner (if related to the claim).

Claim # - The claim number is the insurance company's unique identifier for their file. When talking to the owner or an insurance company, this is the number that they will be familiar with. Many times, the appraisal company will have the ability to look up a file by claim # as well as their file number.

Owner – The owner is very simply the owner of the vehicle. This is who you will contact to set up an appointment (unless the vehicle is at a repair or tow facility or the special instructions say otherwise).

Address – Pay attention to the address column. As simple and straightforward as it may sound, this "should" be the owner's address and where the vehicle is located, but don't take it for granted. Many times, lower down on the assignment sheet, it will give you additional location information. ALWAYS VERIFY THE ADDRESS OF THE VEHICLE LOCATION AT THE TIME OF THE CALL TO THE OWNER.

Phone – Just like the address, additional contact information may be included in the assignment notes. The phone number listed in this first phone column should be the primary contact number, but remember to always look through the entire assignment sheet to verify there isn't a different number you are supposed to call.

It's never a great conversation when you call a separated, soon to be divorced wife, and the husband is mad because you let the ex-wife know he wrecked her car. Especially if it was listed in the assignment notes to NOT CALL THAT NUMBER (true story!).

Vehicle – This will be the vehicle that you have been assigned to inspect. If it belongs to the insured, the insurance company will likely send over detailed information. If it is for a claimant vehicle, you may only receive a brief description. MAKE SURE YOU KNOW WHAT VEHICLE YOU ARE SUPPOSED TO INSPECT.

VIN - VIN stands for, "vehicle identification number". This is the unique identifier of the car. If this is provided MAKE SURE YOU VERIFY the vehicle's

VIN with this. Many times, you will think you are inspecting the right 2012 Mercedes belonging to Mr. Smith only to find out that his wife has the right one, and she took the wrong one on accident (another true story!). The VIN is usually located in the dash or inside the driver's door frame.

License Plate - The license plate is a quick way to identify a car in a parking lot and is a bonus if it is included in the assignment sheet!

Color -The color of the vehicle is also an easy way to help identify a car on the go, but don't rely totally on this. You'd be surprised how many silver Honda Ridgelines with a broken headlight and damage to the left side there are in the same apartment complex! (yet another true story... 3 was how many there were in the same complex with similar damages...).

Damage Notes – This is where the insurance company puts any notes regarding damage they want you as an adjuster/appraiser to be aware of. It usually includes the location of the damage and anything the insurance company wants to be documented or photographed that is unique to this assignment. Once again, don't rely totally on this information. Confirm what the damage are with the owner.

Special Instructions – Not always included with assignment sheets, special instructions can be in addition to the damage notes. If there is a special instructions section, and it includes anything at all, MAKE SURE, YOU PAY ATTENTION!

Client Guidelines - Client guidelines are the insurance company's protocol to you and the appraisal company. These are the specifics of how the insurance company wants you to handle frequently asked questions and situations regarding claims and inspections.

If you need help understanding the guidelines of the assignment you've received, check the chapter in the Playbook (the third part of this book) called "Client Guidelines" for a detailed explanation of many of the common guidelines.

Step 2: Map Out Your Assignment

Being efficient as an IA starts with knowing how to properly map and sort out your assignments.

I recommend segmenting your coverage area into two or three different sections. You'll refine these claim areas or buckets as you handle more claims, but it is important to your cycle time and sanity that you know you can't cover EVERY claim in your coverage area EVERY day.

Segment Your Claims

At first, you'll likely feel like you can drive all over God's green earth for a single claim, but trust me SEGMENT YOUR COVERAGE AREA.

For example, if you cover a single metropolitan area, let's say, Raleigh, N.C., you could segment it into East and West claims. All claims you receive east of Raleigh would fall into the east claim bucket, and all claims west of Raleigh would fall into the west bucket.

You can cover Raleigh "proper" each day, but try alternating which side of Raleigh you cover. This will consistently prevent driving a long way just for a single claim.

Once you have your segments, write down on your calendar what day you'll be covering each area on which day. Alternate back and forth all the way out for two weeks. You can always change your schedule if needed, but what this technique does is give you a handle on when you'll be in a specific area and when, if ever, you need to look forward.

Map Your Claims
With your segments in place, you can now decide what your ideal day for inspecting the claim would be, but before you go calling the owner, I recommend you map all your assignments that you'd like to inspect on that day in a digital mapping program to determine your ideal route.

I highly recommend Badger Maps, although built for salespeople, Badger is AMAZING for inputting your claims in and optimizing your route with a single click.

For less than $20/month it saves your records of assignments, allows you to add notes (what time the owner said they were available, etc.) and manage all your claims. I used it as my claims management system when working as an IA, and it can be managed from a website or from an app on your phone.

Having a digital record of where you need to go makes the job of adding claims on the fly EASY.

Whether you use Badger Maps, Google Maps or MapQuest (yes, that is still a thing… I just looked it up!), map your day out and optimize it to save time and to make sure you won't have to double back over yourself.

Step 3: Status "Claim Received"

Once you finish reviewing an assignment, YOU NEED to go into the appraisal company's assignment portal/management system and status that you have "Received the Claim".

You can usually find this section by clicking on the "status" or "messages" tab within the company's management system. This will show the appraisal company that you are aware of the file, and it will generally give you 24 hours until the next status is required by the appraisal company.

As a dispatcher, I was very impatient and wanted to know if my appraisers were aware of their assignments, and I also wanted to be sure they were able to handle them. Cycle time (or claim completion time) is one of the major measurement metrics that insurance and appraisal companies look at to judge how a company or how an individual appraiser is doing. The dispatcher's job is to distribute files to the appropriate appraisers and to ensure the files are completed on time.

If you set a dispatcher's mind at ease (by letting them know you have received the file) you will earn their trust. There is nothing more frustrating as a dispatcher than waiting 24 hours for a status, calling an appraiser to hear that they were unaware that a file had even been sent to them.

 Once you receive an assignment status "Claim Received".

Scheduling a Day's Work

Having claims lined up that are ready to be inspected is AWESOME, but things can quickly become overwhelming if you don't have a plan of how to schedule your workload.

Most IA's start off with tons of energy, exploding out of the gate to inspect their first few claims within the first few hours of receiving them. They skyrocket up the cycle time ladder and become more and more popular as the IA Firms see quick cycle time and even faster statuses. Then, the long fall back to earth happens...

The new IA starts getting supplements rolling in, they get tired, sick, overwhelmed, or burnt out, and their cycle time starts to suffer. The IA Firm starts to wonder what is wrong and slowly starts to reminisce about how good that appraiser used to be, that is until they hire another appraiser to share the overloaded appraiser's workload. Now the previously overloaded appraiser is struggling to find enough claims and finds themselves adding more companies to increase their volume, which will, in time, serve to only complicate and exacerbate the predicament of being overwhelmed.

This may be a bit of an exaggeration… but not by much. I know because I've been that appraiser and have seen students at IA Path go through this same cycle. Some of the best appraisers I've ever known had IA Firms stop trusting them, wondering what ever happened to their star appraiser.

This is a real thing, and I believe it can be prevented if you have a PLAN… and here is a plan I'd like to present to you. You may find a different plan, or you may change how you schedule, and that is OK. Use my plan to get you thinking, try it out, tweak it, change it, throw it away, but don't ignore the advice of having a plan.

Why I Created a System

I originally designed this system after I had failed completely at scheduling. A tornado had ripped through my hometown and flung hail at every car in its path. It was April 16th, 2011. 37 Tornados in a single day… in a single state. Nearly all in my coverage area.

I received over 100 claims in a single night, and the volume kept pouring in. No matter how much I inspected and handled, I couldn't get in front of my claims for well over two months.

I went from earning $4,000-$6,000 a month to hitting well over $12,000 that next month, and close to it in the following month. In the process, I only slept a few hours a night and lost valuable relationships both professionally and personally. It is one of my true regrets in my business. After that, I knew I needed a plan.

I realized, no matter how HARD I worked, I wasn't enough, and neither will you be. So, let's go over my 4 S's to Stress-Free Scheduling.

4 S's to Stress-Free Scheduling
The key to this system is acknowledging and realizing that putting a status in your files is king! In our business, the one that statuses their files wins... it's that simple. The 4 S's to Stress-Free Scheduling are:

- **Stop** – Stop Inspecting, Stop Running Around
- **Segment** – Segment Your Areas Into Buckets
- **Schedule** – Create Your Schedule
- **Status** – Status ASAP As You GO!

1. Stop
In daily claims, you may need to only stop inspecting for five minutes. If one hundred claims get dumped on

you overnight, you may need to stop for two days, but regardless of how long you stop for, you need to stop and focus on getting a plan together for your new claims.

Many times, we are so concerned with getting the one claim inspected and can't focus on the claims we just received UNTIL we finish those claims. This is OK for a few hours, but you MUST stop and schedule claims FAST. Most IA Firms expect you to acknowledge a new claim within a few hours. STOP and give your new claims for the day their due attention.

Go into each claim you have received and add this status, "Claim Received". Without that status, you may receive "status request" phone calls starting the next morning. With that status, you've just bought 24 hours until the phone calls start coming in… let's make it count!

2. Segment
Once I started doing this, even a little bit, it changed my world. Too often, we as IA's give the vehicle owners the keys to the kingdom by letting them dictate when and where we MUST be. If left uncontrolled, you'll have an owner say,

"Be there between 12:30 and 12:45 because that is my lunch break and the vehicle isn't available at any other time."

This is a recipe for disaster. Especially when this claim is two hours from your previous claim. NO WAY you can guarantee you'll be there in a fifteen-minute window. What if something goes wrong? You then drove two hours for nothing…

This is why we segment and schedule ourselves in certain areas on certain days BEFORE we ever get a claim.

Look at your coverage area and divide it into 2-3 segments. I call these claim buckets.

For most IA's, you'll need two or three claims buckets depending on the size of your coverage area.

Next, write down on your calendar what area you'll cover on which day. Just rotate through each area on alternating days. This is even if you don't have a single claim received. Now, schedule out what areas you predict you'll be in for the next two weeks. That way even if an owner can't meet for a week you know what day you'll be in their area when they are available.

You can always change this later, but I recommend doing this digitally, so you always have access to alter and view this schedule.

As claims come in, you now have buckets/coverage areas to drop them in. This one I can get on

Thursday, this one on Wednesday, so on and so forth.

3. Schedule

Now that you have segmented your claims up, you need to map out your ideal route for each day that your claims fall in. As mentioned before, I use Badger Mapping to keep track of all my claims and to optimize my route. It makes it easy to move claims to a different day and to access my schedule and information ANYWHERE.

Give Windows... not Deadlines

The mapping software will let you key in all the claim addresses so you can see them on a map. This allows you to get an idea of how far they are from each other, which ones should go first, and what order you should do them in. Always put in your starting point (your address) as your first stop which will then give you the time it will take to get to the first claim.

There is also a huge bonus if you use Badger Mapping. You can add in your ending address, either home or wherever you have dinner plans, then you can hit "optimize". Badger Mapping will then give you the best, most time efficient route to handle your claims. This can be a difference between making an appointment and being stuck in Denver rush hour traffic with an upset owner waiting for you.

Depending on which software you are using, you will be able to have information telling you the distance between each stop, the time you will arrive, and you can build in lunch breaks and time for inspections at each appointment.

Now that you have your route information set, you can proceed with calling the vehicle owners.

When you call to schedule an appointment, use the language, "I will be in your area on Thursday between 12-2pm" and be sure you follow up that statement with this statement, "Will your CAR be available?"

Now, why did we give a time range? Why didn't we say "around 12:30?" You know and I know that you said "around" 12:30, but it is likely the owner heard you say that you would be there "by" 12:30. They imagine it as a deadline and not as a window.

I suggest you approach it this way. When making calls, use the type of language I mentioned above: "I will be there between 12-2pm."

You know you'll be there around 12:30 p.m., but if you get delayed, you can still make your appointment. Most owners are OK with this kind of window. Think about it, the cable company, air conditioning company, and pool guy all give windows as big as 12-5pm! Giving a two-hour window is consistently accepted and will save you a huge headache later.

Don't say, "Will YOU be available?" I've had countless conversations with owners trying to figure out a complicated scheduled, just to find out their vehicle is stationary all day at their house. Ask them if their CAR or VEHICLE will be available not them.

These tips will help you, and the customer will feel that the entire appointment setting process is smooth and professional. A good appointment setting process gives the customer an idea of what kind of person you are and sets the tone for the inspection.

For example, if the owner is unavailable on Thursday, you can easily reference your calendar and inform them of the next day you are scheduled to be in that area. This is the beauty of segmenting. You aren't pigeonholed into the one-time slot that MUST work for the owner, they must fit into your schedule.

Will there be times that you must make an exception to get a claim inspected? Sure, but don't make it the normal or you'll deliver bad customer service. You'll have an unorganized scheduled, miss appointments, be late, and all of that is WORSE than telling them if they can't meet on Thursday, you'll be in the area again on Monday.

4. Status
Once you have a scheduled time, even if it is eight days away, STATUS THE FILE. Putting when your

appointment is, stops the phone calls and lets everyone know what is going on with that claim.

IA Firms have told me if they could fix one thing, they would just want us IA's to status better. Don't ignore a file, don't go radio silent, put in a status.

They'd rather you STOP inspecting, SEGMENT your area, SCHEDULE your claims, and STATUS your file than for you to get a few extra claims done today.

HE WHO STATUSES IS KING!

Schedule an Appointment

Now that you have reviewed the assignment, mapped our your day, and input a status for the IA Firm, we are now in a prime position to call the owner of the vehicle to schedule an appointment to inspect the vehicle.

We know where the vehicle is located, that it is in our area, and what type of location the vehicle will likely be at (body shop, tow yard, or with the owner).

If you can't tell, I enjoy giving you simple steps to follow to execute each task with confidence. This is no different. There are 4 steps to making an appointment setting call.

4 Steps to an Appointment Setting Call

Step 1: Review

Open the claim assignment sheet and review the claim information. When the owner picks up, it's normal to have a slight mental blank. That is why reviewing the assignment sheet, verifying the insurance company you represent, the owner's name, and vehicle make, and model can be very important.

I even practice my introduction before placing the call. This makes it more natural when the owner answers.

Constantly look at the assignment sheet while the phone is ringing, focusing on the name of the owner. There isn't a worse way to start making a call than calling an owner by the wrong last name.

When you are certain of the insurance company, owner name, and vehicle click the phone number hyperlink in your Badger Mapping app or be old fashion and dial the phone number on the assignment sheet and be ready for your introduction to the owner.

Two things before you call. Open an internet browser and have one tab open to the Google homepage and one tab on your schedule on a map (Google, Badger, etc.).

Now let's dial!

Step 2: Introduction

You've dialed the owner, and you probably hear a Verizon ringback song of the latest pop star or Sweet Home Alabama... Suddenly you realize that someone just said something. You've blanked! The owner is on the phone, what now?

Well, if you followed the review step, you should have practiced the introduction. I'm going to teach you how to deliver a professional introduction that will let the owner feel like their claim is moving along without confusing them about your role in this process.

When you hear the owner say, *"Hello,"* deliver the follow script

"Hello, my name is Chris Stanley. I'm calling on behalf of XYZ Insurance Company to set up an appointment to inspect and write an estimate on Mr. Smith's 07 Cadillac CTS. Is Mr. Smith available?"

By this point, the owner is aware of your name, who you represent, and who you are looking for. They will usually respond, "Oh yes!", excited to have their vehicle looked at or are already looking for the appropriate person to give the phone to.

From that point, you should have an easy time getting to the owner of the vehicle. If you were not talking to the owner when they arrive on the phone, repeat the same script when the owner comes to the phone (minus the *"is Mr. Smith available?"*).

Then, you will be in a position to get an agreed appointment time.

Step 3: Get an Agreement

You've established you are talking to the owner of the vehicle, and the owner knows who you represent. It is now time to get an agreement for a place and time of inspection. I use the following script:

"Mr. Smith, I'm going to be in your area tomorrow between 9-11am, will your vehicle be available for inspection between 9-11am?"

Make sure you ask if the **vehicle** is available in your window and not if the owner is available. The vehicle may just be sitting at their house and may be available, but if you ask if the owner is available, they may be unavailable, and more than likely you'll cause confusion and not get an easy appointment.

Their response will generally be along the line of, "Yes, I can make that work. It will be at my place of work. It's 5 minutes from my house. Is that OK?"

Your response should be, "That would be perfect. Do you have that address or name of your place of work?

If needed I can look it up online." (Remember those internet tabs?)

If they don't know the exact address type in the name of their business in Google and make sure it's the right location naming the address that comes up along with some key points around it.

If they do know the address type it into Badger Mapping overwriting their address. This is to ensure you don't go to the wrong address tomorrow. TRUST ME DO THIS!

I'd also put in the name column of Badger Mapping the name of their place of work in front of their name (Example: JCPenney Mr. Smith).

Now once they confirm the time will work and you've established the correct address re-confirm both with them.

"Mr. Smith I'll be at your place of work JCPenney' at address 123 Straight Street Aurora tomorrow between 9-11am. If you are available to be present during the inspection that is preferred, but not required."

They will usually say, "That shouldn't be a problem just give me a call when you arrive and if I can come out, I will."

You have just a few more pieces of information that are important to verify: the location, color, make and model of the vehicle.

"Mr. Smith, where do you normally park, and what color is your Cadillac CTS?"

The owner will then usually give very specific instructions of where they park and what color their vehicle is. Type their response into your Badger Mapping notes section for this owner.

"I park on the South side, in front of Taco Bell. My Cadillac is Gold and has a Denver Broncos sticker on the back window."

Now when you arrive the following day, you go to the notes section and immediately know exactly where they park and what to look for.

Close out the conversation by confirming the information once again.

"OK great! I'll come out tomorrow between 9-11am to inspect your gold Cadillac CTS in front of Taco Bell in the JCPenney parking lot. I'll look for the Broncos sticker, and I'll call you once I arrive to see if you can come out."

Congratulations, you have an appointment set.

Go back to Badger Mapping, and in front of work location and owner name, put the abbreviation "CON" for confirmed. Now, you won't wonder if you have an appointment.

Leaving a Voicemail
If you are unable to reach the owner and left a voicemail for them, leave them a voicemail like this,

"Hello, my name is Chris Stanley. I'm calling on behalf of XYZ Insurance Company to set up an appointment to inspect and write an estimate on Mr. Smith's 07 Cadillac CTS. I'll be in your area between 9-11am, please give me a call back at 111-222-3333 to let me know if your vehicle will be available at that time."

Once you have left a message, put a note in Badger Mapping, right in front of the owners name, the abbreviation "LM" to remind yourself that you left a message for that owner. Do not remove them from your route until you haven't heard from them and you must skip their inspection.

Now, let's status the appraisal and insurance company to let them know what we have done on this file.

Step 4: Status the File

Now that we have secured an appointment (or left a message), we need to add a status or message to the appraisal company's online portal.

The same way you put in "claim received" you need to add a status like this:

"Appointment set for 12/16 between 9-11am at the owner's place of work at JCPenney. Owner stated he parks in front of Taco Bell in the JCPenney parking lot."

By putting these details, the insurance and appraisal companies know that you did indeed talk to the owner and set an inspection. If for some reason the owner claims you didn't call or stands you up (and it does happen) and calls to complain, the insurance company or appraisal company can read the status and remind the owner of your conversation.

Once you are finished adding the status, repeat the process until you've gone through all your potential claims.

Status Voicemail Left
If you left a message for an owner, leave a status in the appraisal firms online portal with something along the lines of:

"Left message for the owner on phone number 111-222-4444 at 5:30 p.m. offering an appointment tomorrow morning between 9-11am."

Now you can relax and wait for callbacks or for the next day to arrive. When you receive a call back from an owner, open your Badger Map App to add your notes, confirming times, etc. By using Badger Maps, you can schedule an appointment from anywhere and not lose your notes.

If you can't answer the call, let the owner leave a voicemail, and they usually will let you know if the time slot you offered works or not. Call them back at your first possible chance to secure the appointment.

Now get a good night's rest. Tomorrow we are going to tackle these inspections!

Inspection Conversation

When inspecting a vehicle, there are 3 steps to completing an auto damage inspection.

Inspection Conversation - Having a good conversation with the owner is crucial to understanding the damage and leaving the owner feeling good about the work that you are going to do.

Photos - Taking the required photos and capturing the damage is essential to what you were contracted to do.

Scoping - Proper note taking of the damage and of the conversation with the owner will make the job of writing an estimate and an appraisal report easier for you. The damage notes are called scope notes or "scoping" the damage.

I suggest you complete them in that order. Let's dive further into these steps.

(If you are inspecting the vehicle at a repair shop or a salvage/tow/auction yard, you can reference the chapter on those locations in the Playbook section of this book. We'll only cover inspecting a vehicle with the vehicle owner in this chapter.)

Step 1: Inspection Conversation

When you arrive at the owner's residence or place of work, it's time to have a conversation with that owner. I'm going to go over the 4 key elements of a successful inspection conversation.

Introduction – Just like the phone conversation introduce yourself with your name and the insurance company you represent. Then, offer to look at the vehicle with them. As a personal rule, I try to never go into the owner's house even as a cut through to the garage.

Also, remind them that you will need the car keys to get the mileage.

Their Story – Ask them what happened. They probably have a lot to tell you. Listen carefully to this story. It will probably entail most of the details you will need including the damaged area and the items that the owner is most concerned about.

Take note of anything they say that the insurance company may need to know or would want to be documented.

Confirm the Damage Area – After their story is done, confirm the damaged area.

"Mr. Smith, I see the damage to the front bumper, and I see some scratches on the fender, is there anything I didn't notice that you have noticed?"

This will allow them to point out additional items you may have missed. This makes your job easier, so pay attention.

Set the Expectations – Following confirming the damaged area, let the owner know what the next steps will be.

"Mr. Smith, I'm going to take photos of the entire vehicle, including the damage and take notes. I'll write up an estimate this afternoon and send it to the insurance company. You should hear from the insurance company in the next 48hrs. Do you have any questions?"

This will let the owner have a grasp of what's going on and present them with an opportunity to ask questions. If you are writing the estimate at the vehicle, you would say something like this, "Mr. Smith

I'm going to write up an estimate, and I'll come to get you in about 30 minutes when it's complete."

Taking Photos

Let me tell you a quick story.

Once upon a time, a young appraiser (me) had a large coverage area, 3hrs x 3hrs x 3hrs x 3hrs. After spending a long twelve-hour day of inspections, I sat down to input the damage from the many cars I had looked at. Upon review of the first file, I realized that the very first one could not be completed. The reason why? I had forgotten to take a VIN photo. The owner and I had some great conversation about what had happened, and I simply had gotten distracted and forgotten to take the photo. In the end, this one photo cost me 6 hours of my life re-driving out to the border of my coverage area to re-take that photo and driving back… before sharing photos via cell phone was popular or accepted.

I hope that I can help you never experience that pain in your career.

As an auto damage appraiser or adjuster, there are few tasks we are given that are as easy to judge or be judged on as the photos you take.

When you receive an assignment from the appraisal company. You are contracted to… (at minimum)

1. Document the damage with photos

2. Write an estimate

3. Complete an appraisal report

Both the estimate and appraisal report's validity are judged and based on the photos we upload to the appraisal and insurance company.

Within that assignment that is sent over are guidelines and expectations for you to follow for the claim. This is what must be completed for you to be paid for completing the assignment. Review these guidelines before completing an inspection.

In these guidelines are requirements for photos. Let's look at the most commonly requested photos first.

Standard Required Photos

99% of all files that I have ever completed have requested the following photos:

· 4 Corners (Lt Front, Rt Front, Rt Rear, Lt Rear)

· License Plate

· Vin

· Odometer

· Damage Photos (minimal of 3)

Now, let's go through the standard total loss photos and my recommend photos with an example and a brief description of why each photo can be so important. I will present them in the order I take them in every time. Doing photos in a consistent order and rhythm will ensure THAT YOU NEVER MISS A PHOTO!

You will take all photos, including total loss photos on every vehicle to ensure you never forget to take total loss photos. I make this a requirement for all of my students. We will review the standard photos, then go over total loss photos, but no matter what take all of them!

4 Corners – The 4 corners allow anyone who looks at the photos to see the overall condition of the car. Many times, you will be able to see a majority of the damage, license plate, and prior damage all from just the 4 corners.

The key to getting a corner photo correct is to ensure that you can see one end of the car and one whole side of the car. For example, when taking the left front corner photo, you should stand to the left and front of the vehicle. You should be able to see the entire front and left of the vehicle

I take the photos of the four corners in this order:

Lt Front

Rt Front

Rt Rear

Lt Rear

GAWR RR.: 940 KG
2072 LB

THIS VEHICLE CONFORMS TO
ALL APPLICABLE FEDERAL
MOTOR VEHICLE SAFETY,
BUMPER AND THEFT
PREVENTION STANDARDS IN
EFFECT ON THE DATE OF
MANUFACTURE SHOWN ABOVE.

1N4AL3AP
PASSENGER CAR
MODEL: BDBALP2C60E
COLOR: KH3 TRIM: G

5. License

6. Vin

7. Odometer

8. Dash

License Plate Photo – The license plate photo is good for identification purposes. The insurance company will be able to verify if this is the correct vehicle, and if stolen in the future, have a record of what license plate was on the vehicle they are insuring. It will also provide information regarding when the registration will expire. In the event of a total loss, insurance companies will reimburse owners for the months of taxes they pre-paid.

VIN (Vehicle Identification Number) Photo – The VIN is the unique identifier for the vehicle. The VIN is located in multiple places on the vehicle.

1. Windshield/Dash

2. Driver's Side Door

3. Engine

4. The Frame of the Vehicle

The best VIN photo to take is the one that is located on the driver's door (or on the inside frame or pillar of the door). This will also include the manufacture date which is important when determining the age of the vehicle. This comes into factor when deciding if a vehicle qualifies for alternative parts.

Odometer (or Mileage) Photo – Similar to a timestamp on a photo, this photo is a timestamp of when in the car's life span the insurance company inspected the vehicle. It can be useful in future investigations, but once again, it also can be a determiner or qualifier for A/M or LKQ parts, depending on the insurance company guidelines.

The odometer is in front of the driver, behind the steering wheel, on the dash. In newer vehicles, they are all digital, but older models will be analog.

Make sure when you take a mileage photo that the displayed mileage you are taking a photo of is the "odometer" or "odo" and not a "trip" mileage. I've had this happen more than a few times, and it can be frustrating and embarrassing to call an owner asking them for their current mileage.

If a vehicle's digital dash is displaying the trip, it can be a game of hide and seek to find the correct button to change that to display the odometer. Many owners are not aware of how to change the dash to display the odometer.

Dash Photo – Although not required on all inspections, I highly recommend taking a dash/radio photo after you snap your odometer photo. You only have to move the camera a little and will literally add on 5 seconds to your inspection. This is important in the case of a total loss, because it show a lot of options on the car that could come into question later.

Headliner Photo – Right after I take the dash photo, I point the camera (or phone) up and take a photo of the headliner. This shows the condition of the headliner and also shows if the vehicle has a sunroof. This is very important when a vehicle is a total loss or on hail inspections where performing R/I on a sunroof is a big item to miss. I recommend taking a photo of the headliner on every file.

Driver's Door Photo – Stepping back after the headliner photo, snap a picture of the driver's interior door trim, front seat, and dash. Once again, this shows the condition of the vehicle and a lot of the options that may come into question later if the vehicle is a total loss or a part is needing to be replaced. I recommend doing this on every vehicle.

Damage Photos – Now onto the main event. After having a conversation with the owner, taking all of the "required" photos, you can now move onto the damage of the vehicle. Taking good clear photos is essential to the insurance company. If they can't see it in a photo, they will not want you to write it on an estimate. Don't be afraid to use your finger to point out what you are taking a photo of. I recommend that even if the damage is a small scratch that you take at a minimum the following 3 photos:

1. Looking straight at the scratch

2. One looking from the left of a scratch

3. One looking from the right of a scratch

If the damage is more extensive than a scratch, make sure you take a photo of:

1. Every part that is damaged

2. One of the overall damages from the left

3. One of the overall damages from the right

4. Anything that would justify why you are writing something on your estimate (for example, the hood gap being different from side to side)

I'm adding in a measurement photo. Take a measurement photo of the primary point of impact. Take this photo with the damage photos.
Using a yardstick is an easy way to do this. If you use a measurement tape make sure you put the beginning of the tape (before 1 inch) on the ground and measure up to the point of impact. The insurance company wants to see the measuring tape run from on the ground to the point of impact. Make sure your photo shows the tape or yardstick on the ground for this to count as a proper measurement photo.

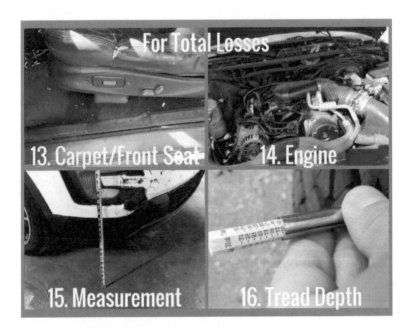

Total Loss Photos

Here are the standard total loss photos for most insurance carriers. Don't forget to also check your guidelines for anything else the insurance company may require.

I recommend you take **ALL PHOTOS INCLUDING TOTAL LOSS PHOTOS on EVERY CAR!**

Carpet/Front Seat Photo – Taking a photo of the carpet and driver's front seat will show the condition and allow for proof of whatever rating you condition the vehicle. The driver's side carpet and seat are the most used part of the vehicle and will usually be the worst reflection of the condition of the vehicle. If the driver's seat has a tear in it that will justify a lower rating on the conditioning chart. Between this photo and the driver's door photo, you will have a proper representation of the driver's seat condition.

Engine Photo – Taking a photo of the engine compartment with the hood up shows how well the vehicle's engine has been maintained. If an engine compartment is sparkling clean, this will justify a higher rating for total loss conditioning or vice versa. After I take the carpet and front seat photo, I'm conveniently located by the hood lever, and it makes it a perfect time to pull it and then walk up front to take my engine photo.

4 Tread Depth Photos – Standard equipment for an auto damage appraiser or adjuster should be a tread depth gauge. You can easily pick one up for a few bucks at any auto parts store.

This gauge shows how much tread is left on the tires. When a vehicle is a total loss, the insurance company uses this measurement to rate the condition of the tires. You only have to provide a rating for front and back, but since you already have the gauge out go above and beyond and snap a photo of the depth of all 4 tires. The key is to put the gauge in the center of the tire to get an accurate reading.

You will NEVER miss photos if you…

1. Read the guidelines before the inspection
2. Take your photos in the same order every time
3. Take all photos, including total loss photos on ALL VEHICLES.

Scoping the Damage

Taking notes of the damage to the vehicle is also referred to as, "scoping the damage". Taking good notes of what damage there is and the operations that will be needed makes it easy to input the damage when you get back to your computer.

Notes also make sure you don't forget anything. I highly encourage writing notes and scoping the damage even if you are going to write the estimate on site. It's hard to hold a laptop, talk to the owner, and get everything into the estimating system simultaneously.

Before you start on the damages write down the VIN number, mileage, license plate, and production date on your sheet.

Below is the 3-step system for taking damage notes.

1. Damaged Panel - Write the damaged panel and the needed operation.

2. Blend Panels - Write the panels that need to be blended with the damaged panel being refinished

3. R/I Operations - Write the items that need to be removed and installed to properly paint all the damaged panels and the blended panels

Use abbreviations to speed up writing. The standard abbreviations are

RR – Remove and Replace for a part that needs to be replaced

HRS – plus the number of hours needed to repair

RI – for items that need to be removed and installed

BL – for items that need to be blended

Just understand that you can use abbreviations to speed things up.

Repair vs. Replace (IA Path Soda Can Rule)

Knowing if a panel needs repaired or replaced is one of the hardest things to master, but it isn't an exact science. To make it easier for you, I came up with the IA Path "Soda Can Rule".

Imagine a damaged panel is a soda can. You can fix a lot of damage on a soda can, but there comes the point where it's cut, and no amount of blowing, pushing or popping will fix it, where you can't restore the shape of the soda can, and it's kinked beyond repair. Think of damaged panels the same way. If you end up being wrong...... IT'S OK!

For more help with Repair vs. Replace, checkout the entire chapter on this topic in the Playbook section in the third section of the book.

Now you at least have a starting point to understand how to look at damaged panels.

Notating Damage
For notating damage start at the main impact point. Write the abbreviation of the repair operations and then the part that is damaged.

Example
- RR Rt Fender

Once you have written down the operation and part, look to see what adjacent panels may need blended (painted in addition to that part for color match. See the "Blend" chapter for help with this).

Example
- BL Rt Front Door

After you are done with the blends, write down all the items that would have to be removed and installed to properly paint both the damaged panel and any blend panels. Write any R/I items underneath the panel they are located on.

I have an Auto Damage Appraiser Inspection Guide in the Playbook section of this book that guides you through all the R&I that is typically needed when a vehicle is being worked. Reference that when needed.

Example
- RR Rt Fender
- R/I Rt Headlight
- R/I Rt Fender Liner
- BL Rt Front Door
- R/I Rt Interior Trim
- R/I Rt Belt Molding
- R/I Rt Mirror
- R/I Rt Handle

Continue with the rest of the vehicle starting with a part that needs repaired or replaced, followed by blends and the R/I.

Once done with that, review your notes and make sure it tells the story of the damages.

Whether you are going to input the damage into the estimating system at the owner's house or back at your office, this method will give you good notes to go back to your computer and input the damage.

Writing the Estimate

We've inspected the vehicle and have everything we need to write up a professional estimate. Don't worry, it isn't as hard as one might think. YES, it is a whole new world to learn, but NO it isn't impossible.

To make it easy I created the **4 Steps to Creating an Estimate.** We'll review the 4 steps and then look at each one individually.

4 Steps to Creating an Estimate

1. Create the File Information

Creating a file for your records that holds.... everything.

2. Input the Claim information

This is the owner's information, claimant information, loss information, insurance company, and any claim details.

3. Input the Vehicle information

Vin, mileage, license plate, color, production date, primary impact point, etc.

4. Input the Damage Information

Inputting all damage that you have notated on your scope sheet followed by the extras needed for repair.

In this chapter, I will go over each step briefly using CCC One as my estimating system of choice.

(If you need assistance with Audatex, please refer to my book, the Audatex Adjuster's Playbook)

Step 1: File Information

The first step of writing an estimate is to create a file in your personal management system. I know what you are thinking, I don't have a personal management system.

The reality is you do! It's powerful, searchable, and best of all free. It's called Windows.

Create a Folder on your desktop called, "Inspections" or "Claims". Now, create a folder inside of the inspections folder for every appraisal company you work for named something like, "XYZ Appraisal Inspections". This will help you keep track of how many claims you have done and for which company.

Every time you get ready to write an estimate create a folder using this template:

File # (appraisal company file #) - City Inspected - Last Name - Vehicle Year & Model - Insurance Company.

When you create a file name, it will look like this:

19545 Denver Smith 09 Altima XYZ Insurance

Now, whenever you receive a call from an owner, adjuster, shop, or appraisal company, you can quickly click the search bar in your laptop and type in the different keywords the caller gives you.

"I'm calling about Mr. Smith's 09 Altima."

Click the search bar and type in Altima. It will bring up a list of files with Altima, but you will probably be able to identify it quickly! If there are too many Altima's on your laptop to see the result, use an additional keyword, along the lines of: 09 Altima or Smith Altima.

Once you have created the folder, unload all of your photos into the file. Every time you have a new document, the estimate, invoice, or a supplement, put the documents into this file folder. You now have a personal claims management system.

 Include your "Inspected" folder in a cloud-based upload service to have your files backed up in the cloud. I suggest Google Drive or Mega (lots of space for FREE!) but Dropbox, Carbonite and others are good as well.

Step 2: Claim Information

The first few screens you will see when starting a new claim in the estimating software is the owner information screen. Depending on whether you are using CCC One, Audatex, or Mitchell, the layout is a little different, but the process is the same.

Take the information you have regarding the owner of the vehicle and input that information.

I have the assignment sheet open on my computer, and I use a keyboard shortcut you should learn, ALT+TAB. This will switch windows on your computer from the estimating system to the assignment sheet quickly.

Highlight the information on the assignment sheet you would like to transfer and use another keyboard shortcut, CTRL+C. This will copy the information.

Click ALT+TAB to switch back to the estimating system. Click the correct field you would like to input the copied information and use the last keyboard shortcut you will need to know, CTRL+V. This will paste the information you copied from the assignment sheet into the correct field in the estimating system.

I fill out the owner information in this order:

- Owner's Name
- Owner's Address
- Owner's Phone Number

In CCC One, on the owner's claim screen, there is also a spot where you select the appraiser, that's you. Select that you are the appraiser and then move on to the claim information.

The next screen will be the information regarding the claim of the vehicle. Don't forget to utilize ALT+TAB to switch between the estimating system and the assignment sheet, CTRL+C to copy information, and CTRL+V to paste.

Make sure you put in the following fields:

- Insurance Company

- Claim # (if you have it)
- Deductible
- Type of Loss
- Date of Loss

The last tab you will be inputting claim information on is the "Inspection Tab". This is where you input all the information regarding your inspection. Fill out the following information:

- Date of Inspection
- Type of Inspection
- Location of Inspection

Once you have filled in all claim information, move on to inputting the vehicle information.

Step 3: Vehicle Information

The vehicle screen has many important fields. Some of the information will come from the assignment sheet while other information will come from the scope sheet that you used during the inspection.

When possible, use the ALT+Tab, CTRL+C, and CTRL+V, if your vehicle information is stored digitally in the assignment sheet. If you don't have it digitally, you'll have to read your notes and type it in yourself.

Let's go through the information you need to fill out on this screen.

VIN – Make sure you input the VIN in correctly at that the system verifies it. The system will tell you if there is an error. If input correctly, the system will identify the Year, Make, and Model of the vehicle. You may be prompted to select an edition if the vehicle has multiple. (example the vehicle is an LS, LT, S, etc.)

Odometer (mileage) – Input the mileage of the vehicle from your inspection.

Production Date – Either from your scope sheet or photos, find the production date.

Exterior Color – Input the color of the vehicle.

License Plate – Once again, from the assignment sheet, photos, or your scope sheet, input the license plate and state.

Primary Point of Impact – Select where the main point of impact took place. If there is a secondary point of impact, select that as well.

Drivable or Not Drivable – The insurance company needs to know if the vehicle can still be driven before repairs. This information will help them when determining rental car days etc.

Prior Damage – If there was some prior damage that you took note of during the inspection, input that information here. Write down where the prior damage was located and describe the damage.

Once you finish with these fields, you can move onto the estimate.

Take note that if you need to update the options of vehicle, it is located on this page near where you put the VIN in as a tab.

Step 4: Damage Information

Inputting the damage information gets the most attention, but really the first two types of information you input into the estimating system are the most important for being compliant with the insurance company. Missed damage is not as big a deal as missing the mileage, putting in the wrong claim number, or putting the wrong VIN in. So focus just as much, if not more attention, on the first two types of information as you do the damage information.

Moving our attention completely to the damage, let's talk about the best way to input damages.

Depending on what the primary point of impact you selected is determines where the estimating software will start you on the estimate. The system isn't perfect, it may start you at the fender instead of the headlights, but just understand that is why it may start you in a specific section.

I recommend that you start at the beginning of your notes and work down. If you are using the IA Path Scope Sheet (and why wouldn't you?) start at the front and work your way back.

Estimating systems are laid out to work front to back on a vehicle. Once you are on the damages or under the estimate tab (when using CCC One), click the "Groups" button located at the far left of the screen about halfway down. This will return you to the part of the system where you select the different sections of the vehicle.

Looking back at our previous examples of a fender being replaced, aka R/R, we had headlights that needed the R/I operation, and the "Front Lamps" section would be a great place to start building our estimate.

Systematically go through section by section, front to back, skipping the sections that have no damaged items, inputting the damages, R/I, and blends, in until you have input all the damage from your scope sheet, notes, and photos.

You'll notice that when you enter a section, there are subsections. To expand the subsections click the + button to the left of the subsection titles to see all the parts in that subsection. Once you navigate through this over and over again, you will begin to memorize where different parts are located inside the system.

If you get stuck and can't find a part, CCC One has a search bar above the sections where you can type in the name of a part to find it. If your search comes back empty, it is because CCC One calls the part you are looking for by another name. Keep your names as generic as possible. Search "Bumper" not "Front Bumper Cover Bracket". CCC One only shows exact matches.

When inputting the damages, keep your photos open, using ALT+TAB to go between the estimating system and the photos to verify what you are inputting. This gives you a last look and quality control before you input the damages.

After all the damages are input, this is when you will put your extras that will be needed for repair into the estimating system (hazardous waste removal, cover car, set up and measure, frame pull).

Once you are complete with the extras, it is important to click on the **Rates tab** to make sure your labor rates are correct. Labor rates are different in each area as are tax rates.

At least have a standard set of rates and taxes that you write the estimate at for your coverage area. You don't want to upload a $0 labor rate. You would get a revision for sure.

Uploading the Claim

With the estimate written, we now need to get our photos, estimate, and notes to the IA Firm or insurance carrier that has hired us. There are **4 Steps to a Completed Claim Upload.**

4 Steps to a Completed Claim Upload

The Estimate - Upload your completed damage estimate

The Photos - Upload your inspection photos

The Appraisal Report - Write an appraisal report/summary

The Invoice - Complete an invoice for both yours and the appraisal company's records

Step 1: Print the Estimate

You've completed your damage estimate, but now you need it to be accessible to the appraisal and the insurance company.

This is a simple process, but some appraisal companies require that you send the actual work file to them through their online portal or through the estimating software. This is usually referred to as an EMS upload. This process varies greatly from company to company, and I will not cover that here. If you work for a company that requires an EMS upload ask your direct contact to walk you through it, check with our **IA Path Community**, or if you are using Audatex, you can refer to my **Audatex Adjuster's Playbook** for the setup and process to do this.

The process is simple enough that you probably will only need to be walked through once or twice to memorize it.

Every appraisal company I have worked for does require a portable document format, aka PDF, copy of the estimate. This is a universal format, and your laptop, tablet, or PC will most likely already have a PDF printer installed on it. If not, a free PDF printer is Cute PDF.

To get a PDF copy of the estimate, click on "Print" the estimate.

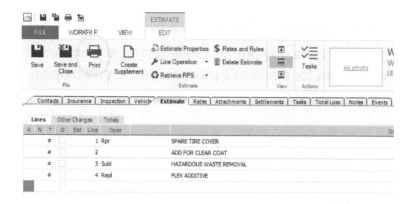

Then select the PDF printer from the list of available printers and click print.

This will allow you to save the printed estimate as a file on your computer. Save it to the claim file that you created along with the photos you have there. This will make it easier on the next step of the upload. Now that your estimate is with the photos we can move on to uploading both the PDF and the photos.

Step 2: Upload the Photos & Estimate

Appraisal company portals differ, but most companies I've worked for make this process simple and as pain-free as possible.

Go to the appraisal company's portal and click the claim that you are working on (If you are following my steps, it is probably open from inputting the claim information).

Click the **file** tab or section from inside the claim and find the upload button. This will usually prompt a search window to appear with the ability to browse your computer.

Navigate either with the search function or by clicking to go to your desktop and eventually your inspections folder.

Locate your claim file on your PC and click on one of the photos or the PDF estimate inside of the file.

Now use the keyboard shortcut, CTRL+A, to select all the files in the folder. On the open window, click the open button to upload all the files you selected (hopefully all of them).

Sit back and wait for the upload to finish. Once that completes, move on to complete the appraisal report.

There are appraisal companies that require you to name your photos. If this is the case, you may have to name the photos before upload on your PC, or some appraisal systems offer a simple naming of the file once it is uploaded. It's up to you to understand the appraisal and insurance company requirements and how to execute with the different companies.

Step 3: Write Your Appraisal Report

The appraisal report is all the information from the estimate, photos, and owner summarized into a short paragraph or two informing the insurance company at a glance what to expect from the file you just uploaded. This is also your opportunity to communicate specific concerns or statements the owner made you aware of.

The appraisal company will either have a place for this appraisal report or expect you to upload a Word or PDF document. I expect most companies will have a place for this information, but if they require a PDF upload, simply complete the appraisal report in a Word document and print it with the PDF printer (similarly to the estimate PDF).

The appraisal report should at least include the following 8 items of information:

1. Date
2. Your Name

3. Owner's Name
4. Vehicle
5. Inspection Location
6. Damaged Items
7. Open Items
8. Owner Notes

Below is the template that I use when creating an appraisal report:

On 11/12, Chris Stanley inspected the owner Mr. Smith's 2009 Cadillac CTS at their residence.

Damaged items include: front bumper cover, absorber, reinforcement, RT fender, and RT headlight.

Open items include front inner structure and possible frame damage.

The owner has concerns about using aftermarket parts.

Using a template like this will help you make sure that you communicate all the necessary and expected information that the insurance company is looking for. It also would be nice to add your own flair of comments to make the template your own. Thank them for the work or for trusting you, have a great week, etc.

Once you write out the appraisal report, either upload it or copy and paste it into the appraisal portal.

Remember to save a copy of the Word document you used into the claim file you created on your computer. This will make for easy reference if you get a call concerning the notes later.

Almost done with this file! We just need to make sure you get paid for your hard work.

Step 4: Create an Invoice

Whether built into the appraisal system, automatic or if you need to send the invoices in batches every two weeks, keeping track of your claims and your invoices IS IMPORTANT. You are running your own business, and if you don't get paid due to your neglect, you have no one to blame but yourself.

When I first started with Nationwide Appraisals, I had never had to turn in an invoice before, and the I.T. and onboarding team assumed I knew what I was doing (because I was up to speed in every other arena with them). I went for two months without pay due to my failure to send in invoices. Don't be afraid to ask how a company wants you to turn in an invoice. This is a normal business question.

Upon submitting, or right before clicking close on a file, you need to document in your accounting software, or at the very least an Excel document, the file you've completed, the appraisal company it is for, the amount you are owed, and some basic claim information for referencing.

I have an invoice template here for you, but I highly recommend that if you start doing some serious volume before you consider getting an accounting software.

If you are considering getting an accounting software, I recommend Fresh Books simply because I like the little guy and it's easy, but QuickBooks is also a great choice.

If you plan on using Excel, head to AutoAdjustersPlaybook.com/guides to download the IA Path version. This will give you a starting point.

I recommend you create a duplicate tab for each company that you work for and then update the name to reflect that company.

Each time you complete a claim, insert a line above the newest invoice. This way your sheet reflects newest to oldest.

When you are paid for a file, turn that line green indicating you know you have been paid for it. This will allow you to keep track of what has been paid for and what hasn't.

The Excel spreadsheet will also allow you to easily keep track of what you are owed and when. This will help you budget and plan for your bills.

In closing of this section I HIGHLY recommend you get an invoicing software and if needed an accountant.

Completing a Supplement

A supplement is an additional payment that is required to cover the entire cost of a vehicle's repairs.

The facility that is repairing the vehicle will submit a supplement request if they find additional damages, additional operations, or part price changes that cause an INCREASE in the final bill.

Now it is our job to determine if the supplement is legitimate, to add the additional items to our original estimate that we created, if need be, re-inspect the vehicle, and upload it to the IA Firm or insurance carrier we are working under for that claim.

4 Steps to a Completed Supplement

1. Review the Supplement
2. Re-inspect the Supplement
3. Match the Supplement

4. Upload the Supplement

Ok, when we left the vehicle last, it was at the owner's residence, damaged. We uploaded the estimate to the appraisal and insurance company and moved on with our lives, looking forward to getting paid for the inspection.

Well, the life of that claim and the owner goes on as well. The owner will want to get the vehicle repaired at a shop of their choice, and whenever the vehicle makes its way into the shop, there will likely be something you missed or couldn't see during the original inspection.

The shop will complete a teardown of the vehicle. A teardown is the process of removing all the parts that are hindering the shop from seeing all the damage the vehicle has. Once the shop completes a teardown of the vehicle, their estimator will go over the damages and will put together a supplement.

A supplement is a revised estimate with additional or supplement items that were originally missed. The shop will then email or fax over their supplement to the insurance or appraisal company. Once they receive the supplement, they will notify you that you have a supplement for your file. It is possible that the shop submit the supplement directly to you, if they do, notify the IA Firm and they will open up the claim for a supplement.

In many ways this process can feel difficult. You rarely are ever paid for a supplement, and the estimate now must be an agreed price with a shop, but rest easy, it isn't that hard.

Let's go over the 4 Steps to a Complete Supplement.

Step 1: Review the Supplement

The great news is the burden is on the shop to prove to you that they need additional parts, labor, and operations. You can ask a lot of questions before the shop feels like you are clueless! If you don't understand why a shop is asking for an item or operation, you can simply ask. That's getting ahead of myself. I just wanted to put your mind at ease.

When you receive, the supplement, download it. It's usually uploaded into the appraisal management system where you uploaded the photos and original estimate. Look to see if the shop sent over any photos or other documents. If any additional documents were included download all images and documents provided.

Open the supplement PDF document and look at the estimate. On the left-hand side of the estimate will usually be an "S1", representing supplement 1, next to all items that were added or changed since your original estimate. This is your roadmap.

Review all the S1 items, review the shop photos if included, and your original photos and see if any items are confusing or you disagree with.

If it all makes perfect sense and the supplemental dollar amount is under $1500, you may not have to re-inspect this vehicle. If it's a large supplement or there are questionable items, you may need to visit the shop within the next 48 hours and re-inspect the vehicle.

If it's a $1500 and under supplement, but no photos were included, call the shop completing the repairs and ask for images and/or invoices to be sent over to support the request for additional items requested.

Review the images and make sure you don't have any questions.

Step 2: Re-inspect the Supplement

If you must re-inspect the vehicle, due to the size of the supplement or items that you disagree with, call the shop and verify the vehicle is on site and ask to speak to the estimator who is handling the file.

Once you arrive, visit the front desk and inform them that you are there to re-inspect Mr. Smith's vehicle and spoke with Matt, their estimator. The shop will ask if you need a copy of the supplement, SAY YES!

When the estimator takes you to the vehicle go through the supplement, line by line, with them there, taking photos of each item on the supplement.

If everything makes sense there on site with the shop, get your photos and let them know you will upload the supplement to the insurance company.

If you and the shop can't come to an agreement, you may need to call your inside adjuster or the appraisal company you are working for, and ask for their guidance, but always try and resolve it between you and the shop.

No matter how you got to this point of the supplement, you now have an agreed repair in a supplement sheet and photos that support those items. GREAT!

Step 3: Match the Supplement

With your agreed repair, go back to your estimating system and open the original estimate that you created for this vehicle. Go to the damages screen (in CCC One) and click "Create a Supplement".

Take the shop supplement and go to the bottom of the supplement. Find the Supplement Summary. This is a list of only the items that were changed, deleted, or added. Make the changes in your estimating software to match the supplement from the shop.

If you can't figure out where a part of the vehicle is located, simply scroll up to the supplement of record where it shows the part groupings on the supplement, and find the part or operation under that grouping.

Once you have completed all the lines of the supplement into your estimating system, review the total dollar amounts and make sure your estimate is the same or close to the shop's final amount.

If there is a large difference, review the labor rates, taxes, and labor hours on the totals page of the supplement versus your supplement in CCC One.

When times get real tough, walk away from the computer then come back to review and go over it again. You need this supplement to be close if not exact!

This will be the amount that the insurance company pays out for the supplement, and the shop will fight for this money if it is far off. In the event you can't match it, email it to the shop and ask them if they will review it and see if you missed anything. They will usually find the items you missed quickly and tell you the difference.

Step 4: Upload the Supplement

Once you feel comfortable with how close your supplement matches the shops, you now go through the process of uploading the supplement, photos, and appraisal report, just like you did your original estimate into the appraisal system.

1. Lock the supplement
2. Print out a copy of the PDF
3. Upload the PDF and photos to the appraisal system
4. Write a Supplement 1 appraisal report
5. Close the file

You've now handled the supplement! Make sure you understand the repairs enough so that if you get a call from the adjuster you can answer their questions. If you don't know the answer to an adjuster's question(s), let them know you will review the file to remind yourself and call them back with the answer.

Review the file, talk to the shop to verify why an operation was needed (if need be) and call back the adjuster with an answer.

Part 2: The Parts

In this section of the book, we'll go over the major parts of the vehicle. This is NOT a comprehensive guide to every part of a vehicle, but rather highlighting the most important and commonly damaged parts of the vehicle.

This section is not a substitute for knowledge, training, or your estimating software, but will help jog your memory or give you a good overview in a hurry.

Ready?

Parts on the Front of the Vehicle

Below is a diagram you can use as a reference when reading this chapter.

1. Bumper

The bumper is made up of three "major" components.

Bumper Cover – What you see in the photo is the front bumper cover. Just like a seat cover or book cover, the bumper cover decorates and makes the front of the vehicle look sleek and nice.

Bumper Absorber - Right behind the bumper cover is a bumper absorber and is made of a foam-like or plastic material. An alternative name you need to know is "Energy Absorber". The foam/plastic can be white or black.

Bumper Absorber Definition - On all late model cars, the energy-absorbing, foam-like material that is situated between the outside bumper cover and the inner bumper.

Bumper Reinforcement - The final piece of the bumper is the actual steel bumper itself. An alternative term for bumper reinforcement is "impact bar".

Bumper Reinforcement Definition - A horizontal bar fixed across the front or back of a motor vehicle to reduce damage in a collision, the final piece is called bumper reinforcement.

Bumper Brackets – Be aware that the bumper cover has bumper brackets on the left and right of the car. There may be more brackets, but just remember, there are a left and a right bumper bracket. Also, whether it's the front or rear bumper the major parts are the same names.

2. The Grille

A grille covers an opening in the body of a vehicle to allow air to enter. Most vehicles feature a grille at the front of the vehicle, and it helps protect the radiator and engine. Merriam-Webster defines a grille "a grating forming a barrier or screen; especially: an ornamental one at the front end of an automobile."

3. The Bumper Grille

Now that you know the bumper and the grille, you probably could have guessed this name. This helps protect the engine, radiator, and condenser while allowing air flow in.

4. Headlight

There are three types of headlights: xenon halogen, xenon, and LED. Halogen is the old-style headlight we all grew up with. Concerning the other types, in estimating you will just really need to know if its halogen or one of the others due to price differences. If you can't tell, turn the car on turn the lights on. If you still can't tell... play rock-paper-scissors and just pick... hopefully the most cost effective one.

5. Fog Lamp

Fog lamps are the small lights, usually lower than your headlights. Fog & Driving Lights illuminate the dark, penetrate the fog, producing bright far-reaching beams of light in front of your vehicle, making driving safer and easy. There really isn't much you need to know other than being able to identify if a vehicle has them or not.

6. Hood Components

Hood - The hood is the hinged cover over the engine of motor vehicles that allows access to the engine compartment. This is the part of the car that you are looking at while you are driving

Insulator - The hood insulator is on the underside of the hood and help keeps the heat off the hood to help the paint from discoloring, suppress engine noise, and also (read this on hotrodders.com), "Those hood liners are also designed to suppress engine fire. The fire melts the tabs, and the liner drops onto the engine giving the passengers an additional few seconds to escape."

Information Labels - These stickers and information labels are on the underneath of the hood. They include emission labels, coolant labels, belt diagrams, etc.

7. Fender Components

Fender - The fender is the American English term for the part of an automobile, motorcycle, or other vehicle bodies, that frames a wheel well. Its primary purpose is to prevent sand, mud, rocks, liquids, and other road spray from being thrown into the air by the rotating tire. It also helps protect the engine compartment during side collisions. The fender is the sheet metal on the right and left of the hood.

Fender Liner - The fender liner is the plastic lining underneath of the fender. This helps keep mud and debris from entering the engine compartment.

Fender Flare - This is the molding around the wheel opening of the fender. Not all vehicles have this, but it can be called a fender flare or fender molding.

8. Windshield Components

Windshield - The windshield is a window at the front of the passenger compartment of a motor vehicle.

Windshield Wipers - Windshield wipers are a motor-driven device for keeping a windshield clear of rain. Typically made with a rubber blade on an arm that moves in an arc.

Windshield Washer Nozzle - Normally located on the hood of the vehicle, the windshield washer nozzle sprays water onto the windshield.

Cowl - The cowl is the part at the rear of the hood, supporting the windshield, that helps properly divert the rain.

Now, we will move on to the side of the vehicle.

Parts on the Side of the Vehicle

Below is a diagram of the parts of the side of the vehicle. Use as a reference for this chapter. May include parts/components represented in other sections.

1. Fender

The fender is the American English term for the part of an automobile, motorcycle or other vehicle bodies that frames a wheel well. Its primary purpose is to prevent sand, mud, rocks, liquids, and other road spray from being thrown into the air by the rotating tire. It also helps protect the engine compartment during side collisions.

The fender is the sheet metal on the right and left of the hood.

2. Wheel

The wheel is made up of two major parts.

Rim - The rim is the "outer edge of a wheel, holding the tire". It makes up the outer circular design of the wheel on which the inside edge of the tire is mounted on vehicles.

Tire - The second component is the tire. A tire is an advanced engineering product made of a lot more than rubber. Fiber, textile, and steel cord are just some of the components that go into the tire's inner liner, body plies, bead assembly, belts, sidewalls, and tread.

3. Door

There are two major parts to the door assembly and other minor parts.

Outer Panel - The doors outer panel or "door skin" is the outer metal layer only.

Door Shell - A "door shell" includes both the outer skin and the door frame and is shipped pre-assembled with the skin already welded and bonded to the door frame.

Handle - Car door handles may protrude from the vehicle's exterior surface or be streamlined into the vehicle's contour. In some automobiles, especially luxury vehicles, the door handles may feature a keyless entry pad, utilizing either a numerical code or thumb scan.

Door Glass - The glass that goes on the door of a vehicle. When rolled down, it is tucked inside of the door on a track.

Weather Strip - The weather strip on a door is a rubber strip that seals the edge of the door to the side of the vehicle.

Belt Molding - The belt molding is located where the door and door glass meet. Think of it as holding up the glass, it is a "belt" after all.

Body Side Molding - Automotive molding or car body side molding are decorative and protective moldings on the car body.

Door Trim Panel - The door trim panel is the interior panel on the inside of the vehicle.

Uniside - The entire side structure of the vehicle is called the uniside. The uniside is also known as the aperture panel. It consists of the Windshield Pillar, Roof Rails, Center Pillar, and Quarter Panel.

4. Windshield Pillar

On either side of the windshield is a vertical pillar. This is the windshield pillar or A-pillar and is the beginning of the uniside.

5. Roof Rail

On either side of the roof, the metal rail or frame above the doors, we will reference as the roof rails. For all intents and purpose, this is a part of the side frame of the vehicle along with the windshield pillar.

6. Rocker

Rocker Panel - The rocker panel is an important part of the uniside of your vehicle. It is located beneath the doors and in between the wheel openings.

Rocker Molding - The rocker molding is a trim piece, usually plastic on the outside of the rocker panel. Not every vehicle has a rocker molding.

7. Quarter Panel Components

Quarter Panel - The quarter panel of the vehicle is located behind the rear doors and before the trunk and rear bumper. It is a part of the structure of the side of the vehicle and is welded on. It usually takes up about a quarter of the vehicle.

Wheel Well Liner - Just like a fender liner, but on the quarter panel, it is usually referred to as the wheel liner.

Fuel Door - The fuel door or gas tank door is only located on one side of the vehicle.

Quarter Glass - Many times vehicles have a small piece of glass above their quarter panels.

Parts on the Rear of the Vehicle

Below is a parts diagram you can use as a reference for this chapter.

1. Rear Bumper

Rear Bumper Cover - Just like the front of the vehicle, the outside of the bumper is the bumper cover.

Rear Bumper Absorber - Behind the cover is the plastic or foam bumper absorber that is either black or white. Just like the front, it can be referred to as an energy absorber.

Rear Bumper Reinforcement - The metal bar that attaches to the rear frame of the vehicle.

2. Taillight

Just like the front of the vehicle or "head" of the vehicle has lights, the back of the vehicle or "tail" of the vehicle has lights called taillights. Many times, there are two sets of lights on the back of the vehicle, one on the deck lid, and one on the quarter panel. Either set is called taillights.

High Mount Stop Lamp – The brake light on the back of the vehicle is known as the "high mount stop lamp". On trucks is it on the back of the cab, SUVs and hatchbacks it is found at the top of the liftgate, and on standard autos, this is found either in the back window or on the trunk.

3. Trunk

Trunk - The trunk, also called a decklid, is the cover for the main area of storage in the back of the vehicle. Many vehicles don't have a trunk or decklid. Trucks, for instance, have a tailgate and SUV's, van's, and hatchbacks have a lift gate.

The easy way to tell the difference is if it's a vertical panel and it lowers, it's a tailgate. If it's vertical and lifts, it's a lift gate. If it has a large horizontal surface, it's a trunk/decklid.

Trunk Lid Trim - Just likes the doors of the vehicle, the decklid, trunk, and liftgate generally all have interior trim panels.

Emblem - Most trunks have the manufacturer emblem located on it. The oval "Ford" is a great example.

Nameplates - Trunks also have nameplates that denote the vehicle model. "Focus" & "LX" are examples of nameplates that could be on the back of a trunk.

4. Back Glass

The back glass of the vehicle is located above the trunk or at the top of the liftgate

5. Muffler

The muffler is at the end of the vehicles exhaust system. Its purpose is to "muffle" the sound of the vehicle.

Parts on the Interior of the Vehicle

Below is a parts diagram that you can use as a reference for this chapter.

1. Door Trim

The door trim is the inside cover of the door. It has the window and lock controls on it.

2. Front Seat

The front seats of the vehicle are usually covered in either cloth or leather. Depending on where you are in the world determines the driver's seat location. Safe to say, the steering wheel dictates which is the driver's seat, and which is the passenger's seat.

3. Rear Seat

The rear seats usually are covered with the same material as the front. They are commonly bench style seats in most types of vehicles.

4. Windshield Pillar Trim (A-Pillar Trim)

The windshield pillar trim covers the inside frame of the windshield pillar. The windshield pillar is frequently referred to as the A-pillar.

5. Center Pillar Trim (B Pillar Trim)

The center pillar trim, or B pillar trim, cover the frame of the B pillar and the inner workings of the seat belts.

6. Quarter Panel Trim (C Pillar Trim)

The quarter panel trim can be a separate piece from the C pillar trim. If you understand that the C pillar trim and quarter panel trim both cover their respective parts, you'll be able to determine if the quarter panel trim is the same or separate from the C pillar trim.

7. Headliner

The headliner covers the interior of the roof of the vehicle. Usually, the headliner is made of a composite material and glued or secured to the inside of the roof.

8. Dash(board)

The dash, or dashboard, contains the instrument panel on modern day cars and is in front of the driver and passenger of the vehicle. Thanks to Wikipedia, we know that originally, the word dashboard applied to a barrier of wood or leather fixed at the front of a horse-drawn carriage or sleigh to protect the driver from mud or other debris "dashed up" (thrown up) by the horses' hooves.

Inner Structure Parts of the Vehicle

Below is a parts diagram you can use as a reference for this chapter.

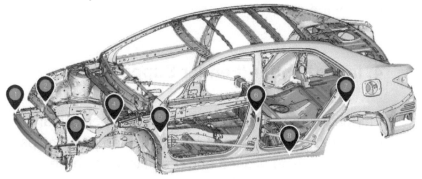

1. Bumper Reinforcement

The bumper reinforcement is connected directly to the frame rail of the vehicle. It is the car's first defense in a front or rear end collision.

2. Radiator Support

The radiator support is the centerpiece of the front inner structure. Many components of the vehicles, including the radiator, condenser, fan assembly, etc. connect to the radiator support.

3. Frame Rail

The frame rail is the frame of the vehicle. The left and the right side has a frame rail, and the frame rail is the core of the car.

4. Inner Fender (Fender Support)

The beautiful exterior of the fender is supported and secured by the inner fender. This framed piece helps keep everything aligned and protects the vehicle during a side or front impact.

5. Windshield Pillar (A-Pillar)

The windshield pillar, or A-pillar, is located at the firewall and dash. Along with the other pillars, the A-pillar helps support the car with vertical support.

6. Center Pillar (B Pillar)

Considered to be the most complex of the pillars, the center pillar or B pillar plays an important role in support, but also in impacts.

7. C Pillar

The C pillar supports the vehicles upper rear and is located behind the rear door before the quarter panel.

8. Rocker Panel

The rocker panel is below the doors of the vehicle and is the lower part of the side structure of the vehicle.

If you take the 3 pillars (A, B, C), the roof rail, and the rocker panel, the entire assembly is referred to as the aperture panel.

Also, there can be an additional D pillar, but this is not as common. (see the images below) As in limousines, there can be additional pillars, but these would be referred to as B1 pillar, B2 pillar, etc.

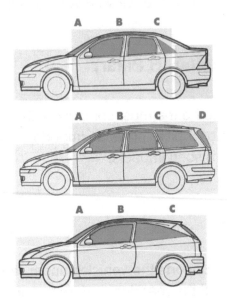

Below is a guide I created to help you identify the inner structure parts of the vehicle easier called, "IA Path's Auto Damage Appraiser's Guide to the Inner Structure of the Vehicle".

You can download your own copy at **AutoAdjustersPlaybook.com/guides**

AUTO DAMAGE APPRAISER'S GUIDE TO
THE INNER STRUCTURE OF A VEHICLE

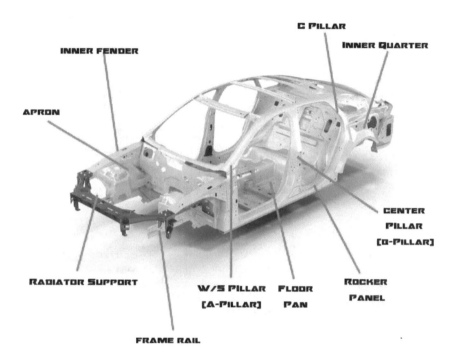

C PILLAR

INNER QUARTER

INNER FENDER

APRON

CENTER
PILLAR
[B-PILLAR]

RADIATOR SUPPORT

W/S PILLAR   FLOOR
[A-PILLAR]   PAN

ROCKER
PANEL

FRAME RAIL

FRAME RAIL

UNISIDE

IF YOU THINK INNER STRUCTURE DAMAGE IS PRESENT ADD

- ALL HITS - SET UP AND MEASURE - 2HRS
- FRONT/ REAR HITS - PULL FRAME FOR MASH/SIDESWAY ETC. - 2HRS
- SIDE HITS - PULL UNIBODY 2HRS LT CENTER/RT CENTER ETC. - 2HRS

IAPATH.COM

115

AUTO DAMAGE APPRAISER'S GUIDE TO THE INNER STRUCTURE OF A VEHICLE

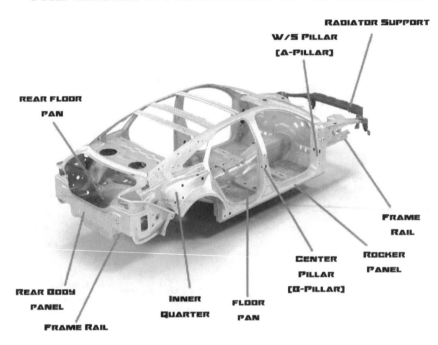

RADIATOR SUPPORT

W/S PILLAR
(A-PILLAR)

REAR FLOOR PAN

FRAME RAIL

ROCKER PANEL

CENTER PILLAR (B-PILLAR)

REAR BODY PANEL

INNER QUARTER

FLOOR PAN

FRAME RAIL

FRAME RAIL

UNISIDE

IF YOU THINK INNER STRUCTURE DAMAGE IS PRESENT ADD

- ALL HITS - SET UP AND MEASURE - 2HRS
- FRONT/ REAR HITS - PULL FRAME FOR MASH/SIDESWAY ETC. - 2HRS
- SIDE HITS - PULL UNIBODY 2HRS LT CENTER/RT CENTER ETC. - 2HRS

IAPATH.COM

You can download your copy at
AutoAdjustersPlaybook.com/guides

Parts That are Involved with Cooling the Car

A real quick blitz on some of the parts of the coolant system. These all are damaged frequently in front end collisions.

Radiator
The radiator is responsible for the cooling of the engine. This is usually located behind the condenser and in front of the radiator support.

Condenser

The condenser is responsible for your air conditioner. This is usually located in front of the radiator.

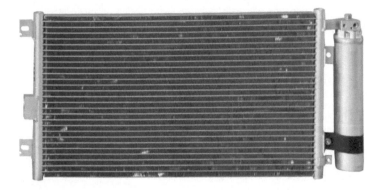

Cooling Fan Assembly

Usually located behind the radiator, the cooling fan assembly and helps the air flow through the radiator and condenser.

Coolant Reservoir

The coolant reservoir is where the radiator's reserve of coolant is located. In a collision, this plastic container is easily broken.

Windshield Washer Fluid Reservoir

The windshield washer fluid reservoir holds the fluid for the windshield washer nozzles to spray out to clean the glass. It too is easily broken being made of plastic. It can be many different shapes and sizes.

Part 3: The Playbook

Some of the content has been used previously in this book, but is also located here to ensure you can find what you need, when you need it.

I go into lots more detail about a lot more things in the Playbook section so make sure you read through these.

This section of the book is broken into small, separate sections to give you quick reference chapters for wherever you are at in the claim handling process.

These smaller sections are:

- **Assignments** – how to get and receive assignments
- **Schedule** – how to schedule claims in your day
- **Inspect** – how to inspect a damaged vehicle
- **Damages** – how to handle and what to look for in specific damage scenarios
- **Total Loss** – how to handle and process vehicles that are a total loss
- **Supplements** – how to handle and process supplements from shops

Part 3: The Playbook: Assignments

Appraiser Pay (Appraisal Rates and Fee Schedule)

This is a topic most IA's love talking about… money. I get asked this question by many of my auto damage students, "What should my appraisal fee be?"

An appraisal fee is how much you charge per claim. In auto, this is typically a flat fee you charge for handling claims in your area. Once you reach a certain distance away you get paid "mileage" based on your agreement with the IA Firm.

Obviously, you own your own business as an IA so I won't tell you what you **should** charge, but rather I'll share what I would do if I were to start over again as a new IA.

We'll cover fee schedules for other types of claims, such as motorcycle as well, only because you'll be asked about it once you apply to your first IA Firm. I'll give you my long-winded answer first, and at the end of the chapter, you will get the complete breakdown of my answers. I didn't just want to hand you dollar amounts, I wanted to explain my logic so YOU can decide what is right for your business.

Appraisal Companies

To gain an understanding of what I would charge if I started over again, I think it would be important for me to point out what the IA Firms are making on a per-file basis.

These firms are running an entire company dedicated to one thing... getting you and other IA's work and supporting you in completing those claims.

They hire salesmen that go around the country talking to clients, they hire full-time Q/C, and office personnel to handle the phones, all while you complete the claim. They absorb a TON of overhead so you can have the opportunity to work a claim.

I start out with that because there are times when we as IA's get cynical and say things like, "Why does the IA Firm make such a big cut? They are just getting in the way!"

In my humble opinion, IA Firms make it possible for you and I to do this job. I personally am not big on traveling to visit an insurance company to land an account, but I'll apply to an IA Firm and complete a claim when I get an email. So, I'm happy to give up a big chunk of the percentage to have a ready-made ecosystem for me to plug into and work.

Typically, IA Firms are making anywhere from $100 (some, a few dollars less) to $125 (roughly) depending on the services and agreements they hold with the insurance company.

I've heard rumors of IA Firms making $200, but that is not normal. The IA Firm you are working for is likely making around a $100. Knowing this we are able to make a good decision about our starting price.

Appraisal Fee

When working as a subcontractor in the PDR industry, the IA field, and a handful of others, I've found that a 60/40 split is pretty standard. Sixty percent to the contractor and forty percent to the firm.

Using this model, I find myself at a $60 appraisal fee. There may be other factors such as the area of the country, competition, skill level, etc. to factor into your appraisal fee, but I believe starting around $60 is what I would do as a new IA.

My goal would be to earn $72,000 a year, and with a $60 price tag, I need to average one hundred claims a month. This is without mileage, any additional fees, or types of claims, but handling 100 claims a month equals 25 a week, which translates to 5 a day. This is a workload I can both imagine getting and being able to handle.

Some firms may ask for less than $60 a file, and if there is a good volume of claims in your area, this can be a great decision, but at least you know what range the fee schedules typically cover.

Whichever way I slice it, I feel confident in my $60 appraisal fee tag, but what about mileage?

Mileage Rate

Gosh, I hate this question, but I'll make it brief. You'll be asked two different questions as it relates to mileage.

1. How many free roundtrip miles do you give with your appraisal fee?

2. What is your per mile fee after those free miles?

With the free roundtrip miles, I've learned IA Firms EXPECT at least 50 and up to 100 free miles. I don't like going 100 miles for free, but I also don't want the IA Firm deciding to use someone else just because I didn't go 60 miles roundtrip for them.

I find myself leaning towards putting 70 miles free and then I simply charge $0.50 a mile. No fancy numbers, just basically the government tax break amount for mileage.

Feel free to play with the numbers, but I've had students get work within a week with those numbers, and they worked out for making a solid living… so I feel good about them.

Quick side note, to get started I drove hundreds of miles in each direction and didn't charge a dime in mileage! I wanted the work so I worked hard for it. This is also an option, but one I'd caution depending on your financial situation as mileage can really add up in a hurry.

Time and Expense Rate (T&E)

Certain claims pay on a time and expense rate, meaning you get paid per hour that it takes.

RV's, heavy equipment, semi's, marine, etc. all typically fall under time and expense. There is no standard database for the parts like auto, and these claims take time to do parts research. Therefore IA Firms pay on a time and expense rate.

Starting out again, I'd start at $40 an hour. This is really low, but I want to get the opportunity to work some of those time and expense claims and would like for the IA Firm to be REALLY forgiving and helpful.

Summary

Thanks for giving me the space to give you such a long-winded answer, I feel it is important that you understand the mindset and not just the numbers, so you can decide for your own business.

Below are the rates that I'd charge for my various appraisal fees if I were to start over again as a new appraiser.

Standard Auto	$60
Photos Only/Cold Call	$30
Time and Expense Rate	$40/hr
Free Miles	70 Free Miles
Mileage Fee (after free)	$0.50/mile
Motorcycle	$90
*This is my fee schedule if I started over again

 | |

Zip Codes and Coverage Area

When you contact IA Firms, they will want to know what coverage area you handle, so having that figured out BEFORE you contact them is a must.

They specifically want to know what zip codes you cover. I remember when I got started spending all day going through zip code maps writing out the zip codes was willing to cover. Heaven forbid I missed one and ended up missing out on claims!

Now, thanks to technology, you can grab all the zip codes you'd like to cover in under a minute.

Zip Codes in Under a Minute

Three steps to get your coverage zip codes in under a minute. It is really this simple and you are welcome in advance for this massive time-saving tip.

1. Visit FreeMapTools.com
2. Select your boundary points on the map
3. Copy and Paste the Zip Codes that are displayed on the screen.

Don't believe its that easy? Watch our video at https://autoforms.co/auto-damage-appraiser-zip-codes/ or head to AutoAdjustersPlaybook.com/guides to find a link.

Now that you know how to get your coverage zip codes, you may still have a few lingering questions about your coverage area. I'll help address those below.

How Big Should My Coverage Area Be?

This is the age-old question, and it really comes down to your specific area and situation. It isn't a perfect science, and it can take some trial and error to get your coverage area where you are satisfied with it, but here are a few things to keep in mind.

Go 100 miles. If possible, be willing to go at LEAST 100 miles round trip. This gives you a 50-mile radius around your home address and the opportunity to earn mileage on claims. Often you can make way more PROFIT off of mileage than you realize, especially if you have a fuel efficient car.

Cover the metro area. If possible, be willing to cover the next large metropolitan area. I lived 1.5 hours south of Raleigh, North Carolina. Raleigh is WAY bigger than my hometown area and provided a bigger flow of claims. I got more in Raleigh than near me, so I was willing to cover the distance.

Go where the work is! Talk with the IA Firms you sign on with. Find out what the closest area they need help is. You can really crank up the volume on your IA business if you fill a desperate need for an IA Firm. I had one company ask me to cover an area on the coast of North Carolina 2 hours from me. I earned mileage on every claim I did out there and tripled my revenue overnight as a result. Plus, the IA Firm felt I had saved them. I was the only IA willing, and I had that area for as long as I wanted it.

Prune when needed. Don't be afraid to quit going to an area if the work there is not consistent and not worth the hassle. There are times to cut off a portion of coverage when the hassle isn't worth the time. Just remember, if the IA Firm needs to find someone else for THAT spot, the new appraiser may dip into your coverage area as well.

Mileage is your friend. There are times when I earned more in mileage than appraisal fees. Earning an extra $50 on multiple files in a day really increases your revenue A LOT! Don't be afraid to drive or extend your coverage area, especially if you can get mileage on those files. Multiple mileage files on the same trip is a great way to increase your revenue as an IA.

Getting Work – The Auto Adjuster's Path

I want to insert a small part from my previous book here, The Independent Adjuster's Playbook. These steps I will unveil work best when they fit within an overall roadmap and strategy in your career.

Just because you apply to an IA Firm doesn't mean they'll hire you, but if you are following the roadmap I provide below, and use the Networking Adjuster's Playbook during the second Phase of your business (shown as the Promoting Phase) you'll be set up for success.

(Excerpt from the Independent Adjuster's Playbook) You may be wondering exactly what steps or tactics you should employ to accomplish your goals in your IA career. You have lots of actions you could take with all the information you've read, but what are the best actions to take that will help you achieve your desired results without walking in circles or wasting steps? Just because you know how to play chess doesn't mean you know how to win.

This is exactly why I created the Roadmap that uses the Independent Adjuster's Playbook to its fullest. I call it the Auto Adjuster's Path. This path is the journey that I have traveled over the last 10 years (and in some cases, what I'd do differently if I had to start over today). The path combines my experiences and knowledge of the industry along with the experiences of other IA's and knowledge from those I've interviewed on the Independent Adjuster Podcast to provide us with a proven map.

3 Phases of the Auto Adjuster's Path
The path is comprised of three phases. These phases each have a milestone for you and your career. As an independent business owner, having a solid understanding of the entire process and the steps that you need to take will bring you confidence.

As you get going and start to find traction, your goals may change and deviate from what I've outlined. Never forget, the Roadmap is to be your guide, not your prison.

This Roadmap is to be your guide, not your prison.

During your journey, you may decide to take a different path than what I've laid out and that is completely fine. This map is designed to help you get started without having a lot of unanswered questions. This is your life, claim it!

In this section, I will go over the phases in a big picture fashion, I cover each step inside of the Independent Adjuster's Playbook in greater detail. If you want a more detailed breakdown of how to do each step that I am about to outline, and wish to grab a better understanding of our industry, grab a copy of that book.

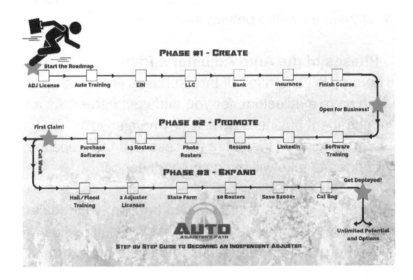

Phase 1: Create Your Business

Phase 1 of the Auto Adjuster's Path is all about **creating your business**. Let's say you were going to start a different type of business, a bakery, for example. You would not only need to know how to bake cakes to have a business, but you would need to create a legal business entity to sell those cakes. Additionally, you would need to have a way to process payments from your customers and have the proper insurance in place. That is what Phase 1 is all about. It includes the following steps:

- Start Auto Training
- Get an Adjuster License
- Obtain Your EIN
- Apply for an LLC (or S-Corp)
- Open a Bank Account
- Get Proper Insurance
- Complete Your Auto Training
- **MILESTONE:** OPEN FOR BUSINESS!

(The MILESTONE at the end of the list of steps lets you know when you have completed the phase, i.e., you know you've finished Phase 1 when you are officially and legally open for business.)

Phase 2: Promote Your Business

Now, if you successfully completed Phase 1, you are officially a business owner. The purpose of Phase 2, going back to the bakery example, is about telling people about the cakes you are selling. So, instead of telling people about cakes, you tell people that you are an independent adjuster and talk about the claims that you can handle.

You must **promote** your business. The steps in Phase 2 are: (This is where the Networking Playbook REALLY comes into play)

- Take Auto Software Training
- Set Up LinkedIn Profile
- Prepare Your Resume
- Get On Photo Rosters
- Find & Join 13 Rosters
- Purchase Estimating Software
- **MILESTONE:** FIRST DAILY CLAIM!

The big milestone in Phase 2 is to earn your first dollar as a claims business. Which is to say, you will know you are done with Phase 2 when you have earned your first dollar in revenue.

Many people may choose to stay here and build their local daily auto claims business. Many people may stay in daily claims forever, but I have a feeling that a majority of people are reading this because they want to pursue catastrophic claims. So, if you want to move on to catastrophic work then move onto Phase 3 ONCE YOU HAVE COMPLETED PHASE 2.

Phase 3: Expand Your Business

Phase 3 is all about expanding your business. By expanding your business, you are no longer just working in Houston, Texas, for example. You are now starting to look to other areas and other states. You are starting to work catastrophic claims. You are expanding the types of claims you are handling. You are moving from just daily collision claims in your area to hail and flood claims around the country. The steps in Phase 3 are:

- Hail and Flood Auto Training
- Two More Adjuster Licenses
- State Farm Certification and Rosters
- 10 Cat Rosters
- $2,000 Storm Fund
- Cat Bag
- **MILESTONE:** FIRST DEPLOYMENT!

Once you get your first call for deployment, you will have completed the final phase of the Auto Adjuster's Path.

Now we return to our regularly scheduled programming and book…

As I mentioned, Kagan Blackburn and I co-authored an entire book on how to get work called the Networking Adjuster's Playbook. If you want to supercharge your work, head over to Amazon (Digital or Physical) of the Independent Adjuster's Playbook (career roadmap and strategy for IA's) and the Networking Adjuster's Playbook (marketing and sales for an IA's).

Guidelines

Below are the most common types of guidelines you will encounter as an independent auto damage appraiser or adjuster.

Guidelines dictate how you can write an estimate based on the company's policies, processes, and procedures. Each client is different and should be treated as such.

Reviewing the guidelines before handling a claim is critical to ensure you meet and exceed your client's expectations.

Client Guidelines - Client guidelines are the insurance company's protocol to you and the appraisal company. These are the specifics of how the company wants you to handle frequently asked questions and situations regarding claims and inspections.

I will go through some of the major guidelines here, but ALWAYS, ALWAYS read a client's guidelines before calling an owner. Some insurance companies have very specific instructions on how they want you to handle their customers and files. I've seen guidelines 6 pages long but read through it!

Photo Requirements - The required photos on the inspection of the vehicle. This can vary on specific photos, but most are the same. We'll cover that more in detail in "the Inspection" section. Just look to make sure they don't require anything specific.

Parts Requirements - Every assignment you will receive will include a guideline for what parts to use when writing an estimate. There are a few major types of parts I'll cover below:

OEM or Original Equipment Manufacturer - When someone says they want "genuine Ford parts" they are talking about OEM Parts. This is the equipment that the manufacturer produces for the vehicle. This is normally the most expensive option, and most insurance companies have guidelines on when you can start using "alternative parts," which is the following part options.

A/M or Aftermarket Parts - A/M or aftermarket parts are non-original parts where someone has replicated the manufactures parts. Think, off brand Ketchup vs.

Heinz. IS THERE A DIFFERENCE? REALLY? Well, in this case, there can be a big difference. The largest and most well know supplier of aftermarket parts is Keystone. There are different certifications and testing that A/M suppliers can go through and most insurance carriers are looking for CAPA Certified A/M parts. As a rule of thumb, I use CAPA certified A/M parts just to be sure I'm following guidelines.

This is a substantial cost saver for insurance companies. Most times insurance companies will have an age or mileage requirement for when you can use aftermarket parts on a vehicle.

Example - 2 years from manufacture date or 12,000 miles.

If there is a requirement like this, and one of the above criteria has been reached you are able to locate the parts, they will likely want you to use aftermarket parts.

LKQ or Like Kind Quality Parts - Like kind quality parts is a nice insurance company way of saying, "used parts". Many times, owners of vehicle don't want "used" parts because they feel their vehicle had "new" parts. That is why the insurance companies decided on this terminology. If a vehicle is a 2006 Ford Mustang and has 120,000 miles you can find an LKQ hood from a 2006 or newer Ford Mustang with less than 120,000 miles to ensure the hood is "like kind and quality."

The owner of the vehicle's hood has 10 years and 120,000 miles worth of wear on it, so the insurance company is obliged to restore him back to his original condition or better.

This can be a cheaper option to OEM and A/M, but not always, so pay attention! **LKQ parts require a 25%** markup when put on an estimate. This is so the body shop can make money on the purchase of a used part. OEM and A/M have that markup built in for the shop to make money.

These are the major types of parts that will usually have guidelines behind them, but you may see guidelines for OEM Surplus or Reconditioned parts, so again, pay attention! This will save you from having a change request sent to you.

Release Estimate - Insurance companies vary whether they want you to send a copy of the estimate to the owner or not. It can also vary if it is a claimant or an insured. There are times when you will be required to email a copy to the owner and other times when releasing that estimate is prohibited. Pay attention to what is expected of you. Many times this guideline is answered with a (Y)es or (N)o.

Total Loss Guidelines - This is where the bulk of the guidelines come into play. When a vehicle has sustained close to its value in damage (75% of value in many states) the insurance company is required to pay 100% of fair market value to the owner of the vehicle and to declare that the vehicle is a total loss. There are many nuances and things that can affect this but understand that if you are close to 75% of the value of the vehicle, then these guidelines will start to come into play.

The guidelines can range from having to take special photos, to checking the oil, getting tread depth of the tires, filling out forms, and calling in the forms to a third-party service that determines the value of the vehicle or to get a salvage bid.

You won't know what you are required to do until you read the guidelines. The total loss process can seem to make claims so much harder, but think of it this way, a car that is total lossed will never have to be re-inspected again..... So, do the total loss process right the first time, and it's likely less time consuming in the long run than a vehicle that is getting repaired and you having to complete a supplement.

The guidelines for an insurance company can vary greatly state by state, so make sure when you are reading the guidelines to see if they have state-specific sections, and you either pay attention to them.... or don't depending on if it is for your state or not.

Status Your Files

If you pay attention to one chapter in this book, please make it this one. **In our industry, you are expected to status a file EVERY 24hrs.** I say a lot of things, but this is something EVERYONE in our industry talks about, but too few IA's apply with vigor.

A status is a digital note updating the IA Firm and insurance company about what is going on with a file.

Typically, this is done inside the IA Firms claims portal. They are usually short and sweet, but it creates a log of the events in a claim. If it isn't in the file as a status/note… it may as well not have happened. When things go wrong on a file, all the status reports are reviewed to determine who is at fault, who dropped the ball, and who is to blame.

This makes me think of something about sailing. When you are sailing, and you think there is potentially big winds or a storm brewing, you can "reef" your sail to make it smaller to make sure you can control the boat even when things get crazy, so you don't end up knocked down! It is a common saying, "Reef early, reef often."

What they are saying is, don't hesitate to pull your sail in if you think something bad is on the horizon. It is better to be prepared. Well I want to give us IA's a new saying,

"Status early, status often."

Listen to me when I say this, your ability to succeed will be directly correlated to your ability to communicate and STATUS in your files. There is a storm brewing on EVERY FILE. No matter how good you are at writing an auto damage estimate, it doesn't matter if you don't communicate to the companies you are working for.

In the beginning, I was a sub-standard auto damage appraiser, but I knew how to status and I was able to overcome HUGE mistakes and problems through status. When I didn't status properly, I often paid the price with big problems.

The number one thing CEO's, claim handlers, and recruiters all tell me is that they wish IA's would be better at providing a status. The number one way to get more claims? Status, status, status!

When to Status?

Remember our saying, "status early, status often". If you think you maybe should status… do IT! Below are the common examples of things you would status in a file. These are in rough order of when they would happen in a claim.

"Received assignment. I will schedule ASAP."

"Appointment set with Mr. Smith for 2-4pm at his place of work, JCPenney on 3/19."

"Left voicemail for owner offering 2-4pm on 3/19 as an inspection time."

"Owner called and canceled the appointment and re-scheduled for 3/20 1-3pm at their place of work JCPenney."

"Owner stated vehicle is at ABC Collision Body Shop at 123 Straight Street Raleigh NC. Confirmed location by calling the shop. Appointment set for 3/19."

"Owner is out of town until 3/27. Appointment set for 3/28."

"Inspected, report to follow."

"Vehicle is a total loss. Will call in the total loss tomorrow during business hours."

"Waiting on part prices from ABC Dealership. Expected within 24hrs."

"Claim will be uploaded by the end of the day."

"Re-opened file. Received supplement from ABC Collision. Re-inspecting tomorrow at the shop."

I could keep going all day, but I think you get the point. Side note, many people in our industry use shorthand status, like this is a text message.

"LM" or "L/M," or "EOD"… what the heck does "please complete by EOD" mean? Oh… it means, "by the end of the day."

I don't believe this communicates much of anything to anyone, "IV hit CV at the DMV. Please inspect IV ASAP." I'm being funny and cynical, I know…

IV = insured vehicle and CV = claimant vehicle, but the point is… THIS ISN'T A TEXT MESSAGE TO YOUR BUDDY!

This document, the log/notes of a file, can be used in a court of law. Communicate properly and don't get lazy and act like it is a text message… it isn't. You don't have to write a book, like my good student Robert did his first week on the job, but you need to write a complete sentence… you are a professional so ACT LIKE IT.

Scheduling Your Status

This is the most important part of your job, communicating through status, and it deserves your attention.

I recommend you schedule time EVERY morning, before you leave to do inspections, to update EVERY open file you have. I can hear you now…

"Chris, that is ridiculous."

UH HUH, but that doesn't mean it isn't a good idea. Remember, our industry expects a status every twenty-four hours. If you don't status and you start inspecting, you'll be receiving at LEAST one phone call for each claim you have that needs a status. Don't make it complicated, make it easy. Status all of them every morning.

Lots of calls don't mean the IA Firm is upset at you, but the dispatcher and file handlers review every file and inform the insurance company of the updates to the files. If the file isn't updated, it is their job to get one.

Save yourself a thousand headaches and phone calls by statusing all your files in the morning. Even if you are repeating a prior status, DO IT!

It also shows you are active in the file and aware that you are assigned it. No one likes a rogue and disappearing appraiser, so remind everyone that you are the best by remembering to STATUS!

Part 3: The Playbook: Schedule

Scheduling a Day's Work

Having claims lined up that are ready to be inspected is AWESOME, but things can quickly become overwhelming if you don't have a plan of how to schedule your workload.

Most IA's start off with tons of energy, exploding out of the gate to inspect their first few claims within the first few hours of receiving them. They skyrocket up the cycle time ladder and become more and more popular as the IA Firms see quick cycle time and even faster statuses. Then, the long fall back to earth happens...

The new IA starts getting supplements rolling in, they get tired, sick, overwhelmed, or burnt out, and their cycle time starts to suffer. The IA Firm starts to wonder what is wrong and slowly starts to reminisce about how good that appraiser used to be, that is until they hire another appraiser to share the overloaded appraiser's workload. Now the previously overloaded appraiser is struggling to find enough claims and finds themselves adding more companies to increase their volume, which will, in time, serve to only complicate and exacerbate the predicament of being overwhelmed.

This may be a bit of an exaggeration… but not by much. I know because I've been that appraiser and have seen students at IA Path go through this same cycle. Some of the best appraisers I've ever known had IA Firms stop trusting them, wondering what ever happened to their star appraiser.

This is a real thing, and I believe it can be prevented if you have a PLAN… and here is a plan I'd like to present to you. You may find a different plan, or you may change how you schedule, and that is OK. Use my plan to get you thinking, try it out, tweak it, change it, throw it away, but don't ignore the advice of having a plan.

Why I Created a System
I originally designed this system after I had failed completely at scheduling. A tornado had ripped through my hometown and flung hail at every car in its path. It was April 16th, 2011. 37 Tornados in a single day… in a single state. Nearly all in my coverage area.

I received over 100 claims in a single night, and the volume kept pouring in. No matter how much I inspected and handled, I couldn't get in front of my claims for well over two months.

I went from earning $4,000-$6,000 a month to hitting well over $12,000 that next month, and close to it in the following month. In the process, I only slept a few hours a night and lost valuable relationships both professionally and personally. It is one of my true regrets in my business. After that, I knew I needed a plan.

I realized, no matter how HARD I worked, I wasn't enough, and neither will you be. So, let's go over my 4 S's to Stress-Free Scheduling.

4 S's to Stress-Free Scheduling
The key to this system is acknowledging and realizing that putting a status in your files is king! In our business, the one that statuses their files wins... it's that simple. The 4 S's to Stress-Free Scheduling are:

- **Stop** – Stop Inspecting, Stop Running Around
- **Segment** – Segment Your Areas Into Buckets
- **Schedule** – Create Your Schedule
- **Status** – Status ASAP As You GO!

1. Stop
In daily claims, you may need to only stop inspecting for five minutes. If one hundred claims get dumped on

you overnight, you may need to stop for two days, but regardless of how long you stop for, you need to stop and focus on getting a plan together for your new claims.

Many times, we are so concerned with getting the one claim inspected and can't focus on the claims we just received UNTIL we finish those claims. This is OK for a few hours, but you MUST stop and schedule claims FAST. Most IA Firms expect you to acknowledge a new claim within a few hours. STOP and give your new claims for the day their due attention.

Go into each claim you have received and add this status, "Claim Received". Without that status, you may receive "status request" phone calls starting the next morning. With that status, you've just bought 24 hours until the phone calls start coming in… let's make it count!

2. Segment
Once I started doing this, even a little bit, it changed my world. Too often, we as IA's give the vehicle owners the keys to the kingdom by letting them dictate when and where we MUST be. If left uncontrolled, you'll have an owner say,

"Be there between 12:30 and 12:45 because that is my lunch break and the vehicle isn't available at any other time."

This is a recipe for disaster. Especially when this claim is two hours from your previous claim. NO WAY you can guarantee you'll be there in a fifteen-minute window. What if something goes wrong? You then drove two hours for nothing…

This is why we segment and schedule ourselves in certain areas on certain days BEFORE we ever get a claim.

Look at your coverage area and divide it into 2-3 segments. I call these claim buckets.

For most IA's, you'll need two or three claims buckets depending on the size of your coverage area.

Next, write down on your calendar what area you'll cover on which day. Just rotate through each area on alternating days. This is even if you don't have a single claim received. Now, schedule out what areas you predict you'll be in for the next two weeks. That way even if an owner can't meet for a week you know what day you'll be in their area when they are available.

You can always change this later, but I recommend doing this digitally, so you always have access to alter and view this schedule.

As claims come in, you now have buckets/coverage areas to drop them in. This one I can get on

Thursday, this one on Wednesday, so on and so forth.

3. Schedule

Now that you have segmented your claims up, you need to map out your ideal route for each day that your claims fall in. As mentioned before, I use Badger Mapping to keep track of all my claims and to optimize my route. It makes it easy to move claims to a different day and to access my schedule and information ANYWHERE.

Give Windows… not Deadlines

The mapping software will let you key in all the claim addresses so you can see them on a map. This allows you to get an idea of how far they are from each other, which ones should go first, and what order you should do them in. Always put in your starting point (your address) as your first stop which will then give you the time it will take to get to the first claim.

There is also a huge bonus if you use Badger Mapping. You can add in your ending address, either home or wherever you have dinner plans, then you can hit "optimize". Badger Mapping will then give you the best, most time efficient route to handle your claims. This can be a difference between making an appointment and being stuck in Denver rush hour traffic with an upset owner waiting for you.

Depending on which software you are using, you will be able to have information telling you the distance between each stop, the time you will arrive, and you can build in lunch breaks and time for inspections at each appointment.

Now that you have your route information set, you can proceed with calling the vehicle owners.

When you call to schedule an appointment, use the language, "I will be in your area on Thursday between 12-2pm" and be sure you follow up that statement with this statement, "Will your CAR be available?"

Now, why did we give a time range? Why didn't we say "around 12:30?" You know and I know that you said "around" 12:30, but it is likely the owner heard you say that you would be there "by" 12:30. They imagine it as a deadline and not as a window.

I suggest you approach it this way. When making calls, use the type of language I mentioned above: "I will be there between 12-2pm."

You know you'll be there around 12:30 p.m., but if you get delayed, you can still make your appointment. Most owners are OK with this kind of window. Think about it, the cable company, air conditioning company, and pool guy all give windows as big as 12-5pm! Giving a two-hour window is consistently accepted and will save you a huge headache later.

Don't say, "Will YOU be available?" I've had countless conversations with owners trying to figure out a complicated scheduled, just to find out their vehicle is stationary all day at their house. Ask them if their CAR or VEHICLE will be available not them.

These tips will help you, and the customer will feel that the entire appointment setting process is smooth and professional. A good appointment setting process gives the customer an idea of what kind of person you are and sets the tone for the inspection.

For example, if the owner is unavailable on Thursday, you can easily reference your calendar and inform them of the next day you are scheduled to be in that area. This is the beauty of segmenting. You aren't pigeonholed into the one-time slot that MUST work for the owner, they must fit into your schedule.

Will there be times that you must make an exception to get a claim inspected? Sure, but don't make it the normal or you'll deliver bad customer service. You'll have an unorganized scheduled, miss appointments, be late, and all of that is WORSE than telling them if they can't meet on Thursday, you'll be in the area again on Monday.

4. Status
Once you have a scheduled time, even if it is eight days away, STATUS THE FILE. Putting when your

appointment is, stops the phone calls and lets everyone know what is going on with that claim.

IA Firms have told me if they could fix one thing, they would just want us IA's to status better. Don't ignore a file, don't go radio silent, put in a status.

They'd rather you STOP inspecting, SEGMENT your area, SCHEDULE your claims, and STATUS your file than for you to get a few extra claims done today.

HE WHO STATUSES IS KING!

Inspecting at Shops, Tow and Salvage Yards

There will be times when you must inspect a vehicle at a tow yard, body shop, or auction and not at the owners residence. Although the inspection is the same, there are different processes and nuances you need to be aware of. I'll cover those in this chapter along with the tips of how I suggest that you interact within these different scenarios, the mindset, and the thought process.

Body Shop

- Ask for a tow bill
- Ask for shop's repair estimate
- Get shop information
  - Address
  - Phone
  - Email
  - Tax ID

o Confirm labor rates

The vehicle can end up at a repair facility that repairs body damage by many different scenarios. The owner could have taken the vehicle there because they trust this shop and want it repaired there, or the insurance company could have had it towed there because they are a part of their repair network.

Just because a vehicle is at a shop doesn't mean they've written an estimate, but while you are there, it DOESN'T hurt to ask if they've written an estimate. This will give you a huge clue to the damages they observed and will help you write a better estimate.

If the shop does have an estimate, use it to guide you through what to take photos of and what to observe. Go through line by line confirming the damage they put onto the estimate. If you don't understand an item, ASK THEM. This is a golden opportunity to write the best estimate possible.

Also, if you don't put it on the original estimate, the shop will likely start repairs as soon as you submit the claim and will send you a supplement. THEN you'll be adding any damages you didn't put on the original, so take the time on an original estimate to look at everything. It'll save you supplemental work later.

The People of the Body Shop

When you first walk into the front of a shop, you will be greeted by someone behind the front desk. This is usually called a customer service representative.

Customer Service Representative (CSR)

This is the first interaction you will have with this shop. I highly suggest you connect and are extremely friendly to the front desk. Many times, they make or break the customer experience at a shop, and the rest of the people at the shop take immediate cues on the CSR's tone and attitude towards you. The CSR has to deal with frustrated customers all day, and this can be very stressful.

The CSR handles most of the incoming phone calls, checking in of customers, dealing with tow drivers, adjusters, appraisers, etc. and if you aren't on their good side, you will have a tough go in a shop. Talk to them, ask them how they are doing, notice how frantic they are working and be aware of what's going on.

Find a point of conversation and strike it up. Once you inform the CSR what vehicle you are there to see, they will get the estimator that is overseeing the repair of the vehicle.

Estimator

The estimator at a body shop oversees the repair of the vehicle and is the liaison from the shop to the owner and insurance company. They communicate updates, newfound damage, part delays, etc. They also work with the body man to ensure that they have an accurate estimate, and they make sure the parts manager orders the correct parts for their repairs.

The estimator is essentially YOU but on behalf of the body shop. Take advantage of this connection and try and relate with the estimator. Discuss the challenges of customers and of the job. You are there to be their friend. You are not the enemy, and neither are they. Work together to make sure what is written is understood by both you and the estimator.

Body Man

The body man is the one who is making the magic happen. He is removing & fixing panels. He is touching the vehicle with his hands for days. He knows the most out of anyone in the shop about the repair that is happening to that vehicle.

Many times, they are not very friendly to appraisers and adjusters. The reason is simple, when a body man asks for repair time to fix a panel, the staff insurance adjuster or appraiser generally negotiates with them to try and save the insurance company money. This upsets the body man because he told

166

them what he needed and now they are trying to negotiate with him, which translates to him making less money.

This is what is going on in the body man's head, meaning he is already defensive and doesn't like you (possibly) because he believes you are going to try and talk him out of money he believes he deserves. Understanding this will help you as you work with the body man. Very rarely do I negotiate with a body man directly; I haven't found this to be something I felt the need to undertake often. Before negotiating, ask him to explain why he needs the number of hours requested and that will usual clear up any confusion you have.

Painter

Painters are the shop money makers or breakers. We don't generally work with painters, but I thought it was important to explain quickly about them. If a shop has a good painter, they are making money. As the cars are being fixed, the painter is making it look like new and the owners are happy. If a painter isn't as good, the entire shop can "bottleneck" at the paint booth.

A bottleneck is when multiple cars that are in the repair process are waiting to be painted and can't move forward in the process until they are finished by the painter.

Body Shop Manager

We don't always deal with the shop manager, but when you do, it's important to remember to be respectful. In the manager's eyes, you are an estimator. He has estimators that work for him and based on that hierarchy, you are below him.
As appraisers, we aren't trying to connect to the manager in the same way we are an estimator. We want to earn respect by giving respect. After multiple visits to the same shop, you will have the opportunity to connect to the manager but rarely does that happen on the first visit.

That is a quick overview of the major roles that people play at a body shop and how you can have an advantage by knowing how to interact with them.

Tow Yard

- Ask for the tow bill
- Ask for storage charges to date

The Tow company is involved when you need to inspect a non-drivable vehicle at a tow yard or when the insurance company or salvage yard contracts them to tow the vehicle to the salvage yard.

The tow companies are usually contracted through the city to be on a rotation. When a vehicle is wrecked within a city or county the next tow company on rotation is called. The vehicle is then stored at the tow facility until the inspection is complete. The vehicle is then either moved to a repair or salvage facility.

When visiting a tow yard, always bring your license and a business card. The tow companies make money not only on towing the vehicle but also on daily storage. This gives them the incentive to find any excuse to not let you, as the appraiser, look at the vehicle. The tow company knows that if it takes you a day or two longer to finish the claim (because you didn't have a business card proving you were an appraiser or adjuster) that is extra money in their pocket.

Most tow companies are not this way, but a few are, and you never know if one is until you have an interaction with one. Many police impound lots are also that way (requiring a license and business card).

When visiting a tow facility, always call ahead and confirm that the vehicle is on site with a name, vehicle, and if possible, license plate and/or vin. The tow yard will confirm that the vehicle is on site.

Once you arrive, visit the office to confirm the location and get a copy of the tow bill and storage charges. Take a picture of this to include with your upload, and add these dollar amounts to your appraisal notes.

The vehicle will not be able to be released to a repair facility until the insurance company pays both amounts.

Salvage and Auction Lots

Auto auctions purchase total loss vehicles from the insurance companies, owners, and car lots and resell them.

There are instances as an auto damage appraiser where you will have to inspect a vehicle at a salvage lot or auto auction.

When a vehicle is at an auto auction or salvage lot, always call and confirm that the vehicle is at the location. It can take up to a week for a vehicle to be transported to one of these locations. When speaking with a salvage or auction lot, they will have a lot number that they identify the vehicle with. They usually also verify the vehicle using the last six of the VIN (vehicle identification number).

There can be hundreds or thousands of cars on site, and on days that the auctions are live, it can be pure chaos. Always confirm if you are able to inspect the vehicle at the time you will be there and ask if they can pull the vehicle up to the inspection lot for you.

Many of the lots require the insurance company to verify that you personally are coming to inspect the vehicle. When you call to confirm the location of the vehicle, make sure you are cleared to inspect the vehicle. If not, you will have to contact the insurance or appraisal company to get them to call and give you authorization.

Upon arrival, visit the office and check-in. They will give you a bright colored vest to wear while going in the inspection lot.

Once your inspection is completed, let them know so they can move the vehicle back to its designated row.

The major Auto Auctions are

- Copart USA (Copart)
- Insurance Auto Auction (IAA)
- Manheim Auto Auction

How to Complete a Cold Call or Photos Only Inspection

There will come a day when you are asked to complete a photos-only claim or a "cold call". You may be wondering what that means… and I'd say, good question.

I've had students come back after receiving IA Path's Auto Damage Certification with that very question their first week on the job, so this chapter made the cut!

Below is the definition of a cold call that I liked best. I found this definition on BusinnessDictionary.com (slightly modified for our purposes).

"Calling a prospect (who does

not know the caller) for an appointment. Also called cold canvassing."

Cold calling is when you show up to a house that the owner is unaware that you are coming in an attempt to make contact or to inspect their vehicle, all in the hopes that the vehicle or owner will be present.

What Do I Charge for a Cold Call?

It is standard to charge your photos-only rate for a cold call inspection. I've done cold calls for twenty-five dollars, thirty dollars, and thirty-five dollars, but typically it comes down to your photos only pricing agreement.

It can be a totally separate agreement for cold calls, so make sure before you complete a cold call you understand what you'll be getting paid before completing the inspection.

When Do I Do a Cold Call?

Another great question, I recommend you do a cold call as an auto IA ONLY when asked by an insurance company, OR it is along your daily route and it would benefit you if you could inspect that vehicle today versus another day.

Cold calls can be uncomfortable if the owner is home, and I've had some bad experience with cold calling, including being chased off the property by a gun... SERIOUSLY!

So, I advise caution on showing up to someone's property without their knowledge, and ALWAYS approach with caution, going directly to the front door and not sneaking around looking for a vehicle. Attempt to look for the owner before doing anything.

Completing a Cold Call

If you are attempting a cold call, I can assume you have attempted to contact the owner on multiple occasions via phone and email (if available) and left messages.

To complete an industry standard cold call, there are a few boxes you need to check to get paid for a cold call visit (whether requested or voluntary).

 Typically, IA Firms and insurance companies DON'T PAY for cold calls unless they requested you to complete it. You are rolling the dice for your own benefit otherwise.

Completing a Cold Call With the Vehicle On Site

If you complete a cold call and the vehicle is on site, Eureka! Knock on the door to see if the owner is home and inform them of who you are and what you are doing. Complete your inspection as normal and move along with your door.

If the owner is NOT present, you may choose to take photos of the vehicle, but don't attempt to open the vehicle. Stick to the exterior of the vehicle and take photos of the interior through the windows.

Do this fast, you will be faced with an uncomfortable and suspicious owner if they come home to see you "sneaking" around their vehicle. Also, neighbors can present fun conversations.

I suggest you leave a business card/note at the resident's door and on the vehicle. This is just one last attempt to make contact.

Completing a Cold Call Without the Vehicle On Site

There will be cold calls that are like dead ends... with nowhere to go, you will need to document that you did indeed attempt a cold call.

First, you'll want to take a picture of the house. Back up enough to show the yard and other houses, so it is undeniable what house you were at. Don't just take a close up of a door... that doesn't tell anyone anything.

You'll also need to get a picture of the mailbox/address on the house showing you went to the correct address they had listed on the assignment sheet.

Lastly, you'll want to take a picture of the street signs that show the closest cross street. AGAIN, we want to prove we went to the correct location or inform them that the address they gave is NOT correct or the vehicle was not at home.

If you do those three things you've successfully completed a cold call, below is a summary list of how to complete a cold call inspection.

1. Picture of house and yard
2. Picture of mailbox/address on the house
3. Picture of closest cross street signs

Photos-Only Claim

A photos-only claim is just like it sounds. You are hired to do EVERYTHING you normally do on an inspection, but you don't have to complete a digital estimate on the vehicle.

Still, take the full photo set, write down damage notes, complete an appraisal report and upload the claim as you normally do. You just skip writing the estimate in Audatex or CCC One.

Items You'll Need for a Photos Only Claim
- Photo Set
- Damage Notes
- Appraisal Report

Part 3: The Playbook: Inspect

Taking Photos

Let me tell you a quick story.

Once upon a time, a young appraiser (me) had a large coverage area, 3hrs x 3hrs x 3hrs x 3hrs. After spending a long twelve-hour day of inspections, I sat down to input the damage from the many cars I had looked at. Upon review of the first file, I realized that the very first one could not be completed. The reason why? I had forgotten to take a VIN photo. The owner and I had some great conversation about what had happened, and I simply had gotten distracted and forgotten to take the photo. In the end, this one photo cost me 6 hours of my life re-driving out to the border of my coverage area to re-take that photo and driving back… before sharing photos via cell phone was popular or accepted.

I hope that I can help you never experience that pain in your career.

As an auto damage appraiser or adjuster, there are few tasks we are given that are as easy to judge or be judged on as the photos you take.

When you receive an assignment from the appraisal company. You are contracted to… (at minimum)

1. Document the damage with photos

2. Write an estimate

3. Complete an appraisal report

Both the estimate and appraisal report's validity are judged and based on the photos we upload to the appraisal and insurance company.

Within that assignment that is sent over are guidelines and expectations for you to follow for the claim. This is what must be completed for you to be paid for completing the assignment. Review these guidelines before completing an inspection.

In these guidelines are requirements for photos. Let's look at the most commonly requested photos first.

Standard Required Photos

99% of all files that I have ever completed have requested the following photos:

· 4 Corners (Lt Front, Rt Front, Rt Rear, Lt Rear)

· License Plate

· Vin

· Odometer

· Damage Photos (minimal of 3)

Now, let's go through the standard total loss photos and my recommend photos with an example and a brief description of why each photo can be so important. I will present them in the order I take them in every time. Doing photos in a consistent order and rhythm will ensure THAT YOU NEVER MISS A PHOTO!

You will take all photos, including total loss photos on every vehicle to ensure you never forget to take total loss photos. I make this a requirement for all of my students. We will review the standard photos, then go over total loss photos, but no matter what take all of them!

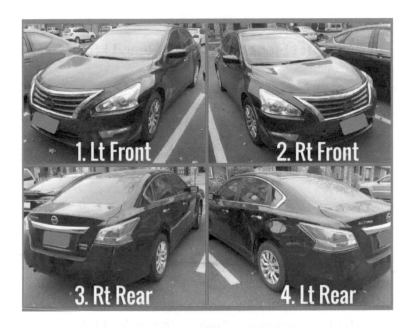

4 Corners – The 4 corners allow anyone who looks at the photos to see the overall condition of the car. Many times, you will be able to see a majority of the damage, license plate, and prior damage all from just the 4 corners.

The key to getting a corner photo correct is to ensure that you can see one end of the car and one whole side of the car. For example, when taking the left front corner photo, you should stand to the left and front of the vehicle. You should be able to see the entire front and left of the vehicle

I take the photos of the four corners in this order:

Lt Front

Rt Front

Rt Rear

Lt Rear

License Plate Photo – The license plate photo is good for identification purposes. The insurance company will be able to verify if this is the correct vehicle, and if stolen in the future, have a record of what license plate was on the vehicle they are insuring. It will also provide information regarding when the registration will expire. In the event of a total loss, insurance companies will reimburse owners for the months of taxes they pre-paid.

VIN (Vehicle Identification Number) Photo – The VIN is the unique identifier for the vehicle. The VIN is located in multiple places on the vehicle.

1. Windshield/Dash

2. Driver's Side Door

3. Engine

4. The Frame of the Vehicle

The best VIN photo to take is the one that is located on the driver's door (or on the inside frame or pillar of the door). This will also include the manufacture date which is important when determining the age of the vehicle. This comes into factor when deciding if a vehicle qualifies for alternative parts.

Odometer (or Mileage) Photo – Similar to a timestamp on a photo, this photo is a timestamp of when in the car's life span the insurance company inspected the vehicle. It can be useful in future investigations, but once again, it also can be a determiner or qualifier for A/M or LKQ parts, depending on the insurance company guidelines.

The odometer is in front of the driver, behind the steering wheel, on the dash. In newer vehicles, they are all digital, but older models will be analog.

Make sure when you take a mileage photo that the displayed mileage you are taking a photo of is the "odometer" or "odo" and not a "trip" mileage. I've had this happen more than a few times, and it can be frustrating and embarrassing to call an owner asking them for their current mileage.

If a vehicle's digital dash is displaying the trip, it can be a game of hide and seek to find the correct button to change that to display the odometer. Many owners are not aware of how to change the dash to display the odometer.

Dash Photo – Although not required on all inspections, I highly recommend taking a dash/radio photo after you snap your odometer photo. You only have to move the camera a little and will literally add on 5 seconds to your inspection. This is important in the case of a total loss, because it show a lot of options on the car that could come into question later.

Headliner Photo – Right after I take the dash photo, I point the camera (or phone) up and take a photo of the headliner. This shows the condition of the headliner and also shows if the vehicle has a sunroof. This is very important when a vehicle is a total loss or on hail inspections where performing R/I on a sunroof is a big item to miss. I recommend taking a photo of the headliner on every file.

Driver's Door Photo – Stepping back after the headliner photo, snap a picture of the driver's interior door trim, front seat, and dash. Once again, this shows the condition of the vehicle and a lot of the options that may come into question later if the vehicle is a total loss or a part is needing to be replaced. I recommend doing this on every vehicle.

Damage Photos – Now onto the main event. After having a conversation with the owner, taking all of the "required" photos, you can now move onto the damage of the vehicle. Taking good clear photos is essential to the insurance company. If they can't see it in a photo, they will not want you to write it on an estimate. Don't be afraid to use your finger to point out what you are taking a photo of. I recommend that even if the damage is a small scratch that you take at a minimum the following 3 photos:

1. Looking straight at the scratch

2. One looking from the left of a scratch

3. One looking from the right of a scratch

If the damage is more extensive than a scratch, make sure you take a photo of:

1. Every part that is damaged

2. One of the overall damages from the left

3. One of the overall damages from the right

4. Anything that would justify why you are writing something on your estimate (for example, the hood gap being different from side to side)

I'm adding in a measurement photo. Take a measurement photo of the primary point of impact. Take this photo with the damage photos.
Using a yardstick is an easy way to do this. If you use a measurement tape make sure you put the beginning of the tape (before 1 inch) on the ground and measure up to the point of impact. The insurance company wants to see the measuring tape run from on the ground to the point of impact. Make sure your photo shows the tape or yardstick on the ground for this to count as a proper measurement photo.

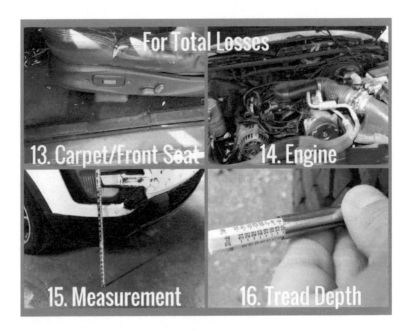

Total Loss Photos

Here are the standard total loss photos for most insurance carriers. Don't forget to also check your guidelines for anything else the insurance company may require.

I recommend you take **ALL PHOTOS INCLUDING TOTAL LOSS PHOTOS on EVERY CAR!**

Carpet/Front Seat Photo – Taking a photo of the carpet and driver's front seat will show the condition and allow for proof of whatever rating you condition the vehicle. The driver's side carpet and seat are the most used part of the vehicle and will usually be the worst reflection of the condition of the vehicle. If the driver's seat has a tear in it that will justify a lower rating on the conditioning chart. Between this photo and the driver's door photo, you will have a proper representation of the driver's seat condition.

Engine Photo – Taking a photo of the engine compartment with the hood up shows how well the vehicle's engine has been maintained. If an engine compartment is sparkling clean, this will justify a higher rating for total loss conditioning or vice versa. After I take the carpet and front seat photo, I'm conveniently located by the hood lever, and it makes it a perfect time to pull it and then walk up front to take my engine photo.

4 Tread Depth Photos – Standard equipment for an auto damage appraiser or adjuster should be a tread depth gauge. You can easily pick one up for a few bucks at any auto parts store.

This gauge shows how much tread is left on the tires. When a vehicle is a total loss, the insurance company uses this measurement to rate the condition of the tires. You only have to provide a rating for front and back, but since you already have the gauge out go above and beyond and snap a photo of the depth of all 4 tires. The key is to put the gauge in the center of the tire to get an accurate reading.

You will NEVER miss photos if you…

1. Read the guidelines before the inspection
2. Take your photos in the same order every time
3. Take all photos, including total loss photos on ALL VEHICLES.

Repair Operations

Everything that needs to be done to repair a damaged vehicle needs to be written down, step by step, in the form of an auto damage estimate. We group the types of repairs that need to be done into different types of repair operations. Every line of an estimate will include a type of repair operation.

Below is a definition of a repair operation.

"Repair operations are types of processes and labor that need to happen to restore a vehicle back to pre-loss condition."

The different types of repair operations are the cornerstone to understanding how to write a proper estimate. This makes understanding the different types of repair operations essential to our job.

In this chapter, I'll dive into the major repair operations to make sure you understand of each one.

Replace

AKA – RR, REPL, Remove and Replace

This may be the easiest one to understand, so we'll start here with a definition for the replace repair operation.

> *"Replace is when you throw a part away and 'replace' it with another one."*

When you determine that a part cannot be re-used or repaired, then you must **replace** it. There are times when this decision is easy, such as a broken headlight, but it isn't always a straight-forward decision.

Also, once you decide a part needs **"replaced"**, your work isn't done. There are different types of parts, and you must determine which part type to use based on your guidelines, cost, and expertise. We'll cover that in a later chapter titled, "Replacement Part Types", but I wanted to mention the list of major part types here.

OEM – Original Equipment Manufacturer
LKQ – Like Kind & Quality
A/M – Aftermarket
Recon/Reman – Reconditioned or Remanufactured

Remove & Install

AKA – R/I, RI, R&I

When a vehicle is being repaired, many things need to be removed and installed. These items don't have to be damaged, but they need to be moved for some reason so a proper repair can take place. Below is my definition.

> *"R&I represents taking something off the vehicle and putting it back on after the vehicle has been repaired."*

This item may need to be removed because it is damaged and needs worked on, but the work must be done off the vehicle. It may need to be removed so the repair shop can access something behind it. It may need to be moved so a panel can be painted without painting over an item etc.

The point is, we use the remove and install operation a lot, and it is important to truly understand it. To make sure you get how the remove and install operation is used, I'll give my favorite example I teach my students of the **Auto Adjuster's Crash Course.**

R&R vs. R&I

To clear up any confusion you may have between **Remove and Replace** and **Remove and Install**, I'd like to use a household example. We are going to write an estimate on a damaged television remote.

The remote is no longer working, and you suspect that the batteries are to blame... now as the repairer you must **replace** the batteries. We'd write the estimate like this.

Repl - Batteries - 2x - $2.50 - .2
(operation) – (Part) – (Quantity) – (Price) – (Labor Hrs)

Simple enough right? Well, if all you are ONLY authorized to replace the batteries, you'll be unable to complete the repair.

There is something in your way... the battery access cover. There is NOTHING wrong with the battery cover, but it is in the way. It must be **removed** and once the batteries are replaced **installed**. We now need to add this line to our estimate,

RI – Battery Access Cover - 1x - $0.00 - .1
(operation) – (Part) – (Quantity) – (Price) – (Labor Hrs)

There is no part cost for removing the battery access cover, only labor is needed.

Although we've only written two lines on the estimate:

Remove and Replace – Batteries
Remove and Install – Battery Access Cover

We have communicated 4 steps which must be done to complete the repair.

1. **Remove** Battery Access Cover
2. **Remove** Dead Batteries
3. **Replace** Batteries With New Ones
4. **Install** Battery Access Cover

That is why the operations are **Remove and Replace** and **Remove and Install**. It is indicating two steps for each of these repair operations.

Repair

AKA – RP, Rpr, Conventional Repair, CR

When a damaged part doesn't need to be replaced, and can be saved, we utilize the repair operation. This one you could have probably figured out yourself, but the repair operation isn't JUST confined to repairing a damaged part. Let's look at the definition, and I'll explain further.

> *"This represents a corrective repair to a part to avoid replacement or any labor needed to get a vehicle back to pre-loss condition."*

Typically, repair is associated with body filler (such as Bondo), but it can also be other methods to correct an existing part on a car to pre-loss condition.

A great example of this is glass cleanup. There is technically no specific part damaged (other than the replaced glass), but the glass needs cleaned up from the vehicle. Labor must be performed, and this labor doesn't fall into Remove and Install or Replace. Repair indicates that to restore the vehicle back to pre-loss condition someone MUST clean up the glass.

The cost to repair a part, or perform a repair operation, is calculated based on the number of hours it is predicted to take.

These hours are represented through whole numbers and tenths of an hour with decimals (.1), and it is important to point out that repair hours are subject to the appraiser, adjuster, shop, repair technician, and insurance company's judgment, expertise, experience, and negotiation.

This brings me to two VERY important IA Tips:

 **A repair can be completed faster than the hours indicated due to the skill of the technician.**

 **There is no "right" repair hour number. It is subjective.**

Refinish

AKA – RF, Ref, Refn

Refinish is the repair operation for painting a panel. It can include other things such as sanding and prepping, but you can almost swap the term refinish and paint, but the technical and repair operational term is "refinish".

Below is my definition for the refinish operation.

> *"Refinish is a labor operation that represents repainting a panel or preparing a panel for paint."*

The labor given to refinish is calculated based on the number of hours it is predicted to take to perform the operation. These hours are represented through whole numbers and through tenths with decimals (.1).

The good news with refinishing is that, as IA's, we don't have to decide how much labor time is needed to paint a panel. The auto repair industry has databases that determine the number of hours an average technician can perform the given refinish operation.

Unlike the "repair" operation, refinish is generally not negotiable and is provided within the industry standard estimating database software.

The estimating systems determine the number of refinishing hours needed when "repair" or "replace" is selected on a panel.

Blend

The repair operation "**blend**" is the kid brother to refinish. This represents painting a panel then blending or overlapping the color into the adjacent panel to avoid color match problems.

> *"Blend represents painting a panel then blending or overlapping the color into the adjacent panel(s) to avoid color match problems."*

Why do we blend? Great question. Let's go back to a household example.

Imagine your spouse has asked you to repaint a wall in the living room where the nephew ruined it with a permanent marker. It has been years since the room was painted. You start out with the intention of only painting one wall, but after completing the one wall, you realize how bad the walls next to it look. One looks shiny and new, the others not so much.

You end up chasing the new paint look around the room and paint the entire room.

The blend operation is designed to help with this issue when a panel is getting painted. We blend the refinish operation into the next panel, so it isn't obvious only one panel was fully painted.

Blend Guidelines

There are certain situations when you choose to blend and others when you don't. For the most part, it is straightforward, but like many things in our industry, there are many opinions as to the "right way" to choose how to blend.

I will stick by widely accepted guidelines and try to make it as easy as possible on you.

When considering if a panel needs "blended", you have to determine FIRST if the car qualifies for blend. What this means is that not all paint colors need blended, and then the SECOND thing you need to determine is if the panel that you are considering a blend operation on qualifies for blend.

This may sound ambiguous, but I'll give you 3 questions to ask yourself that will make it easy. The first two rules are to help you determine if the CAR qualifies as a vehicle that will possibly need blending, and the last one is to help you determine if the PANEL you are considering does indeed need blending.

1. Does the *vehicles* paint have metallic in it? (car)

2. Is the *vehicle* paint light in color? (car)

3. Does the *panel* share a horizontal plane with a panel being refinished and not have a large gap between the panels? (panel)

If you answer YES to the first question (metallic in the paint) then you can skip the second question and assume the vehicle qualifies for blend.

Cars with metallic in the paint always qualify for blend

Metallic is the metal specks or flakes in the paint. I personally call them sparkles, but technically it is called metallic.

If there is NO metallic in the paint you ask the second question, "Is the vehicle light in color?"

Except for white, all vehicles that are light in color will qualify for blend.

If the vehicle does not have metallic in the paint and is not light in color, I do not recommend applying blend on the first inspection.

Many body shops and repair facilities write estimates based on the rule that the only colors they don't blend are white and black. As an IA, I've had MANY files rejected for blending dark colored vehicles which, in turn, has made me develop the above guidelines, but understand that a shop will likely request blend on a dark color vehicle.

They aren't WRONG, we just operate under different guidelines. Check your guidelines for the carrier you are working for when faced with that situation.

Sublet Repair

This represents a repair that the repair facility will typically "subcontract" out to another company to complete.

The types of repairs and companies that are utilized vary greatly from mechanical operations to window tint, cleaning, paintless dent repair, hazardous waste removal and more.

The important thing to remember about sublet repair operations is that they are usually only a price. Labor hours are not used with sublet repairs.

Think of it as a receipt. You are paying off a receipt or quoted invoice for the work the repair facility will have to have done.

Now I want to touch on some of the major types of sublet repairs.

Mechanical Repairs

Some body shops can't or don't do mechanical repairs. This means engine and transmission replacement/repairs are often written up as sublet repairs.

Scanning, airbag reset, alarms, and diagnostics are many times sent to the dealer and can be a sublet repair operation.

Wheel operations, such as alignment, mounting, balancing, etc. are typically sublet repair as well.

Paintless Dent Repair (PDR)

Paintless Dent Repair (or PDR) is how hail damage and minor dents can be repaired without painting a panel.

This is accomplished by massaging the dent from the underside of the panel, or if no access is available, using a technique called a glue pull.

PDR is usually written up as a sublet repair and will be a sublet repair operation you will be very familiar with if you work a hailstorm.

The PDR cost is based on the industry standard price matrix. This matrix allows you to identify the price based on the number, size, and location of the dent.

We have an entire chapter later in this book on writing hail repairs if needed.

Specialized Repairs

Body shops specialize in auto body repair. Many times, they don't specialize in certain things that need to be done to fix the vehicle completely back to pre-loss condition

Window tint and install, decals, stripes, and upholstery repair are common types of specialized sublet repairs.

Hazardous Waste Removal

Every vehicle that is painted has extra paint and materials that need to be properly disposed of.

Hazardous waste removal companies are hired by the repair facility to pick up and dispose of their hazardous waste.

We write this on every estimate that has a panel being painted as a sublet repair line.

Scoping the Damage

Taking notes of the damage to the vehicle is also referred to as, "scoping the damage". Taking good notes of what damage there is and the operations that will be needed makes it easy to input the damage when you get back to your computer.

Notes also make sure you don't forget anything. I highly encourage writing notes and scoping the damage even if you are going to write the estimate on site. It's hard to hold a laptop, talk to the owner, and get everything into the estimating system simultaneously.

Before you start on the damages write down the VIN number, mileage, license plate, and production date on your sheet.

Below is the 3-step system for taking damage notes.

1. Damaged Panel - Write the damaged panel and the needed operation.

2. Blend Panels - Write the panels that need to be blended with the damaged panel being refinished

3. R/I Operations - Write the items that need to be removed and installed to properly paint all the damaged panels and the blended panels

Use abbreviations to speed up writing. The standard abbreviations are

RR – Remove and Replace for a part that needs to be replaced

HRS – plus the number of hours needed to repair

RI – for items that need to be removed and installed

BL – for items that need to be blended

Just understand that you can use abbreviations to speed things up.

Repair vs. Replace (IA Path Soda Can Rule)

Knowing if a panel needs repaired or replaced is one of the hardest things to master, but it isn't an exact science. To make it easier for you, I came up with the IA Path "Soda Can Rule".

Imagine a damaged panel is a soda can. You can fix a lot of damage on a soda can, but there comes the point where it's cut, and no amount of blowing, pushing or popping will fix it, where you can't restore the shape of the soda can, and it's kinked beyond repair. Think of damaged panels the same way. If you end up being wrong...... IT'S OK!

For more help with Repair vs. Replace, checkout the entire chapter on this topic in the Playbook section in the third section of the book.

Now you at least have a starting point to understand how to look at damaged panels.

Notating Damage
For notating damage start at the main impact point. Write the abbreviation of the repair operations and then the part that is damaged.

Example
- RR Rt Fender

Once you have written down the operation and part, look to see what adjacent panels may need blended (painted in addition to that part for color match. See the "Blend" chapter for help with this).

Example
- BL Rt Front Door

After you are done with the blends, write down all the items that would have to be removed and installed to properly paint both the damaged panel and any blend panels. Write any R/I items underneath the panel they are located on.

I have an Auto Damage Appraiser Inspection Guide in the Playbook section of this book that guides you through all the R&I that is typically needed when a vehicle is being worked. Reference that when needed.

Example
- RR Rt Fender
- R/I Rt Headlight
- R/I Rt Fender Liner
- BL Rt Front Door
- R/I Rt Interior Trim
- R/I Rt Belt Molding
- R/I Rt Mirror
- R/I Rt Handle

Continue with the rest of the vehicle starting with a part that needs repaired or replaced, followed by blends and the R/I.

Once done with that, review your notes and make sure it tells the story of the damages.

Whether you are going to input the damage into the estimating system at the owner's house or back at your office, this method will give you good notes to go back to your computer and input the damage.

Replacement Part Types

When choosing to replace a part, it isn't as straight forward as just saying it needs to be replaced. The estimating software will force you to choose what TYPE of replacement part is going to be used.

Understanding the different types of replacement parts and what they mean in plain English will help you meet your guidelines, explain the different types to owners, and talk intelligently with the shops you will be interacting with.

To make this practical and easy for ANYONE to understand, I'd like to use the analogy of a cell phone. Most of us understand that there are multiple types of phones to purchase, so we'll use an iPhone as an example to explain the different types of replacement part types.

OEM (Original Equipment Manufacturer)

When you see the abbreviation OEM, this represents the ORIGNAL manufacturer of the parts/vehicle. For example, if an owner says, "I want Honda parts", they mean they want OEM parts.

Cell Phone Example - OEM = buying an iPhone from the Apple Store brand new. It is untainted and most importantly Apple. It is OEM.

LKQ (Like Kind and Quality)

LKQ parts are used parts. No one likes the term "used" and like kind, and quality better describes what type of part must be used.

You can't just use ANY used part, you must use a used part that is the same like, the same kind, and the same quality of the part being replaced before the loss.

Need a used engine? Well, it needs to be the same year or newer and has the same or fewer miles than the one being replaced.

Currently, LKQ Corp is the main supplier of LKQ parts and what most shops use to order their parts.

If you need to locate used parts, I recommend Car-Part.com.

Cell Phone Example – Buying an LKQ phone is like buying a cell phone off Craigslist or eBay. It is USED.

A/M (Aftermarket)

OK, now we get to some fun stuff. Most vehicle owners do not enjoy getting aftermarket parts. They may look like the OEM counterparts, but they are made by a different manufacturer, and at times there are issues with how they fit on the vehicle.

Keystone (owned by LKQ Corp) is the main supplier and provider of aftermarket parts for most vehicles. You can locate the aftermarket parts often through your estimating software (CCC One or Audatex) and also you can visit orderkeystone.com.

Keystone has a line of certified parts that they call CAPA Certified, which guarantees quality and fit. I recommend you only use CAPA Certified aftermarket parts but check your guidelines.

Cell Phone Example - Aftermarket parts are like an iPhone knock off. It may look the same, may even feel the same, but Apple didn't make it. Just like with phones, the parts many times have qualities that make them less desirable than OEM parts, but it is very common to write for aftermarket parts.

Recon (Reconditioned) or Reman (Remanufactured)

Recon and Reman parts are parts that have been fixed, re-done, or improved... meaning there was something wrong with them and now there isn't.

These are not as common as the others listed above, but some guidelines and situations do dictate that you should look for these types of parts.

You can locate some of these types of parts through Napa for mechanical or Keystone for rims. Also, inside of the estimating software they can be listed as well.

Cell Phone Example – Our iPhone has stopped working, and we file an insurance claim. They send back a "refurbished" phone from Asurion (or whatever your phone insurance company is). It isn't new, it is used, but touched up. This is comparable to the Recon and Reman parts.

Repair Hours Guide – How to Determine Repair Hours

Writing a professional estimate requires an understanding of what is the industry standard expectations of how many hours are needed to repair a damaged panel.

I created a repair hour guide for my students that allow them to take an educated guess on how many repair hours were needed on a panel and not feel like they didn't understand the rules to the game. This helped them "bluff" the first few times until they had the confidence to realize they REALLY did know enough to decide the number of repair hours.

How can we decide how many repair hours are needed? Before I give you the repair hours guide, I want to recap the "repair" operation that this is used for.

Repair

AKA – RP, Rpr, Conventional Repair, CR

When a damaged part doesn't need to be replaced, and can be saved, we utilize the repair operation. This one you could have probably figured out yourself, but the repair operation isn't JUST confined to repairing a damaged part. Let's look at the definition, and I'll explain further.

"This represents a corrective repair to a part to avoid replacement or any labor needed to get a vehicle back to pre-loss condition."

Typically, repair is associated with body filler (such as Bondo), but it can also be other methods to correct an existing part on a car to pre-loss condition.

A great example of this is glass cleanup. There is technically nothing damaged, but the glass needs cleaned up. Labor must be performed, and this labor doesn't fall into Remove and Install or Replace. Repair indicates that to restore the vehicle back to pre-loss condition someone MUST clean up the glass.

The cost to repair a part, or perform a repair operation, is calculated based on the number of hours it is predicted to take.

These hours are represented through whole numbers and tenths of an hour with decimals (.1), and it is important to point out that repair hours are subject to the appraiser, adjuster, shop, repair technician, and insurance company's judgment, expertise, experience, and negotiation.

This brings me to two VERY important IA Tips:

 **A repair can be completed faster than the hours indicated due to the skill of the technician.**

 **There is no "right" repair hour number. It is subjective.**

IA Path Repair Hours Guide

While there is no "right" repair hour number, there is an industry standard and accepted "range". This can feel overwhelming when you are just starting out. No one wants to be the new green appraiser that walks up and writes a two hours repair when it is a ten-hour dent.

To help you get a handle on what number of repairs should be, I created the IA Path "Repair Hours Guide".

I initially used this with my students from our certification course, and they found it INVALUABLE! I decided to share it within this book so you can feel the confidence they felt from not having to guess.

I break damages into 4 different categories, and all that you are left with deciding is which of these categories the damage falls into. You then use that measurement to determine how many labor hours are needed.

- **Nick** (less than 1 inch) - 0.5 hours
- **Scratch** (more than 1 inch) – 1 hour
- **Dent** – 2 hours
- **Impact** – 1 hour for how many "fists" you would need to cover the affected area of the dent

I expect that while you are looking at damages that you use your "adjuster" hat to make decisions. If a scratch is 1 hour, but you have twenty scratches on a door from an angry girlfriend keying a car… this doesn't mean twenty hours!

Use common sense to adjust accordingly. This doesn't excuse you from making a judgment call but is merely a starting point to making your decision.

Below are some examples of each type of damage. REMEMBER, the software will automatically include the refinish/paint time on the damage panels. You are just writing repair hours for fixing the damage before being painted.

Nick

This damage where the bumper and fender meet is a nick of damage on each panel. I would write .5 hours of repair time on BOTH the bumper and fender.

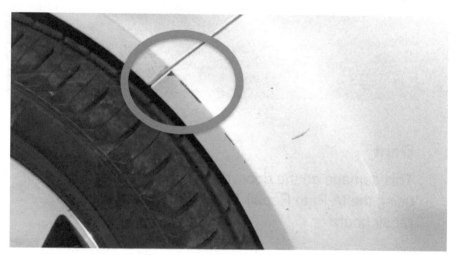

Scratch

Below is an example of the damage that would fall into the "scratch" category. I'd be writing 1 repair hour on the bumper.

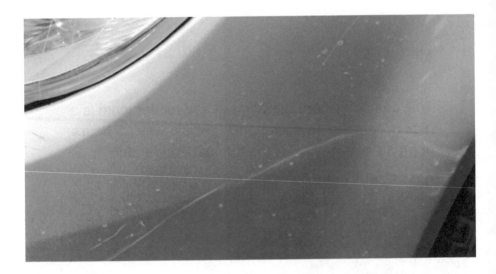

Dent

This damage on the door, I'd classify as a "dent" using the IA Path Repair Hours Guide and write 2 repair hours.

Impact

While much of the damage to this vehicle obviously needs replacement, the damage to the left front door of this vehicle is NOT. I would be considering repair on this panel, and I would need to use our "impact" measurement on the IA Path Repair Hours Guide.

I'd be using my first to measure how many fists it'd take to cover the damaged area. When using this measurement, It roughly takes eight fists to cover this affected area so I'd write an eight hour repair. Some may simply replace this door, and that is an OK decision, but this is to show how to use the repair hour guide on a large dent.

Creases Cause Increases

The last thing you'll need to consider with the IA Path Repair Hours Guide is creases in the damage.

When a panel is creased, it is MORE difficult to restore back to pre-loss condition. Remember that paper airplane you made as a kid and got the crease wrong? Good luck getting it flat again... right? Metal that has been creased is VERY difficult to repair, and we'll need to think seriously about whether to replace a panel or not based on a crease.

If you decide to repair a panel that has a crease determine the number of repair hours needed based on the Repair Hours Guide and then DOUBLE it. That is how much harder it is to repair a crease.

Make sure you confirm it is cost effective to repair when compared to just replacing the panel.

Below are some examples of creases on a metal panel.

While this may only appear to be a 3-4 hours' worth of damage on this panel by our repair hours guide, I'd be doubling it due to the creases causing increases in repair time and writing 6 repair hours.

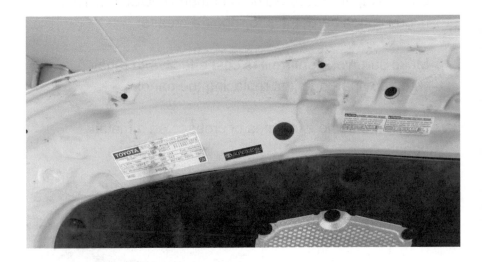

This yellow hood has a serious crease on the edge of the hood. It may only appear to be a 2-3-hour dent, but I'd be writing 6 hours to repair it. Due to the complexity of repair, it may need to be replaced, but if you'd write 6 hours repair based on the repair hour guide and remember that "creases cause increases" and double your number, you'll be in the industry acceptable repair hour range.

Max Repair Hours

At IA Path, I can't stand ambiguous things like, "whatever is cost-effective", because we are often forced to make a snap decision, and we don't always know what is cost-effective at that moment. That is why I'm a huge fan of guides. So, for this book, I decided to come up with a new guide.

I call it the Max Repair Hours Guide. This is the max amount I usually put on a panel before replacing. This will give you an idea, at a glance, if the number of repair hours you are thinking warrants replacement consideration, part by part. There may be exceptions if a parts cost is exorbitant, but what is shown below is for typical situations.

Part	Max # of Hours
Bumpers	6 hours
Hood	8 hours
Fenders	6 hours
Doors	8 hours
Uniside/Aperture/Pillars	12 hours
Roof	15 hours
Quarter Panel	10 hours
Decklid	8 hours

Repair vs. Replace

Few things are more difficult when you get started as an auto damage appraiser than deciding if a part needs to be replaced or can be repaired.

We are often filled with self-doubt and unsure of ourselves. Know that this is normal and that just because you aren't sure doesn't make you stupid.

The ability to properly determine what needs replaced and what needs to be repaired comes with time and experience. To help you gather experience without looking like a newb, I do have some guidelines and rules you can use to make the decision process easier.

1. Cost Comparison - It Is All About the Money

As a general rule, the insurance company wants you to choose the most COST EFFECTIVE and safe repair to restore a panel back to how it was before it got damaged (pre-loss condition). This gives us our first determiner for whether a part needs to be replaced or repaired.

If it would cost more to repair than to replace you can simply replace the part.

2. When in Doubt... Throw It Out

If you have any doubt in your mind, replace the part. Most IA's underestimate damages. Rarely have I seen an IA that either nails the amount of damage or one that overestimates, so I'd encourage you to lean toward replace more than repair.

This will save you many supplement items. I've noticed that I am one of the IA's who underestimates and has regretted trying to repair panels. Nothing like kicking yourself in the butt because as soon as you send in your completed file, you have a supplement to replace that part.

My father-in-law is a MASTER of not getting supplements and justifying his damages with photos and notes. We all can aspire and try to learn from his example.

 When in doubt throw the part out.

3. IA Path Soda Can Rule

When I first started teaching others how to write estimates, I knew as an instructor that I needed to give my students more than "well you just know…" on when to replace or not. I thought long and hard about how I decided what to throw away and what I decided to give the repair operation a try.

I remember clearly how a lightbulb went off in my head, and I ran to my wife like I had just won the lottery. It was at that moment I came up with the IA Path "Soda Can Rule".

The metal on a vehicle that has been damaged MUST be repaired and restored back to the condition it was before the loss... right? Well imagine that the panel you are inspecting is an empty soda can that you damaged and now needs to be restored back to pre-loss condition.

You can blow inside that soda can. You can manipulate the metal by popping this side and pushing it over here. If it was a soda can could you fix it and reuse it?

There are a few obvious things that thinking this way tells use. First off if the can has a SHARP CREASE it is nearly impossible to fix that soda can. Panels on a vehicle are the same way (metal or plastic bumpers).

If the metal is CUT, it is nearly always a part that needs to be replaced. So, the IA Path Soda Can Rule is this,

 TIP   **If this panel was a soda can... can you fix it?**

4. Max Repair Hours

At IA Path, I can't stand ambiguous things like, "whatever is cost-effective", because we are often forced to make a snap decision, and we don't always know what is cost-effective at that moment. That is why I'm a huge fan of guides. So, for this book, I decided to come up with a new guide.

I call it the Max Repair Hours Guide. This is the max amount I usually put on a panel before replacing. This will give you an idea, at a glance, if the number of repair hours you are thinking warrants replacement consideration, part by part. There may be exceptions if a parts cost is exorbitant, but what is shown below is for typical situations.

Part	Max # of Hours

Bumpers	6 hours
Hood	8 hours
Fenders	6 hours
Doors	8 hours
Uniside/Aperture/Pillars	12 hours
Roof	15 hours
Quarter Panel	10 hours
Decklid	8 hours

Blend Guidelines

The repair operation "**blend**" is the kid brother to refinish. This represents painting a panel then blending or overlapping the color into the adjacent panel to avoid color match problems.

"Blend represents painting a panel then blending or overlapping the color into the adjacent panel(s) to avoid color match problems."

Why do we blend? Great question. Let's go back to a household example.

Imagine your spouse has asked you to repaint a wall in the living room where the nephew ruined it with a permanent marker. It has been years since the room was painted. You start out with the intention of only painting one wall, but after completing the one wall, you realize how bad the walls next to it look. One looks shiny and new, the others not so much.

You end up chasing the new paint look around the room and paint the entire room.

The blend operation is designed to help with this issue when a panel is getting painted. We blend the refinish operation into the next panel, so it isn't obvious only one panel was fully painted.

Blend Guidelines

There are certain situations when you choose to blend and others when you don't. For the most part, it is straightforward, but like many things in our industry, there are many opinions as to the "right way" to choose how to blend.

I will stick by widely accepted guidelines and try to make it as easy as possible on you.

When considering if a panel needs "blended", you have to determine FIRST if the car qualifies for blend. What this means is that not all paint colors need blended, and then the SECOND thing you need to determine is if the panel that you are considering a blend operation on qualifies for blend.

This may sound ambiguous, but I'll give you 3 questions to ask yourself that will make it easy. The first two rules are to help you determine if the CAR qualifies as a vehicle that will possibly need blending, and the last one is to help you determine if the PANEL you are considering does indeed need blending.

 **1. Does the *vehicles* paint have metallic in it? (car)**

2. Is the *vehicle* paint light in color? (car)

3. Does the *panel* share a horizontal plane with a panel being refinished and not have a large gap between the panels? (panel)

If you answer YES to the first question (metallic in the paint) then you can skip the second question and assume the vehicle qualifies for blend.

 **Cars with metallic in the paint always qualify for blend**

Metallic is the metal specks or flakes in the paint. I personally call them sparkles, but technically it is called metallic.

If there is NO metallic in the paint you ask the second question, "Is the vehicle light in color?"

 **TIP** **Except for white, all vehicles that are light in color will qualify for blend.**

If the vehicle does not have metallic in the paint and is not light in color, I do not recommend applying blend on the first inspection.

Many body shops and repair facilities write estimates based on the rule that the only colors they don't blend are white and black. As an IA, I've had MANY files rejected for blending dark colored vehicles which, in turn, has made me develop the above guidelines, but understand that a shop will likely request blend on a dark color vehicle.

They aren't WRONG, we just operate under different guidelines. Check your guidelines for the carrier you are working for when faced with that situation.

Auto Damage Appraiser Inspection Guide

WARNING! This chapter may make you feel like a superhero saving the day with auto claims, it may make this entire job feels so easy that you fall so in love with this book that your spouse gets jealous... proceed with caution.... YOU'VE BEEN WARNED.

It is great to read an entire book on auto damage, but when it comes time to looking at a vehicle and remembering what is most important... it can be overwhelming.

When do you blend? What do I need to remove and install? Did I miss any pictures?

These are questions that will come flying up. I know it did for my students. That is why I created the Auto Damage Appraiser Inspection Guide.

This is a single sheet of paper you can put on your clipboard and have all the standard processes you need to consider when refinishing a panel, blend guidelines, photo requirements, plus my repair hours guide all on a single sheet.

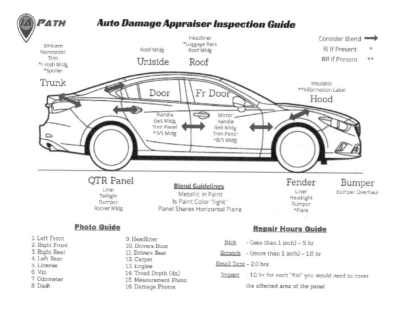

How to Use the Auto Damage Appraiser Inspection Guide

There is a lot of information on this single page, but it can be broken down into 4 different sections/guides.

1. R&I, Refinish and Blend Guide

The picture of the vehicle has all the major exterior parts that typically get painted. You can see the list below.

- Bumper
- Hood
- Fender
- Roof
- Uniside
- Front Door
- Rear Door
- Quarter Panel
- Trunk

With each of those major parts are the items you either need to R&I, or in the case of the hood, "information labels" replace when refinishing a panel.

In the top right is a legend that explains what the symbols mean.

* = R&I If present (meaning, not every vehicle has this part)
** = R&R if present
--> = Consider Blend

Let's do an example. You are looking at damage on the front door of the vehicle. You know it needs repaired and then obviously refinished, but you don't remember everything that needs to be R&I'ed.

According to this to this, you should R&I the following items,

- Mirror
- Handle
- Belt Molding
- Trim Panel
- * B/S (Body Side) Molding * = if present

Now you know what is typically removed and installed when a door is damaged.

Also, we can look at the consider blend arrows and see that it is telling us to consider blend on the rear door and fender. That brings us to the next part of this guide.

Blend Guidelines

Once you know you need to consider blending a panel, use the blend guidelines to determine if THIS car and THAT panel you are considering qualify for blend using the rules listed.

When considering if a panel needed "blended", you must determine FIRST if the car qualifies for blend. What this means is that not all paint colors need blended, and the SECOND thing you need to determine is if the panel that you are considering a blend operation on qualifies for blend.

This may sound ambiguous, but I'll give you 3 questions to ask yourself that will make it easy. The first two rules are to help you determine if the CAR qualifies as a vehicle that will possibly need blending, and the last one is to help you determine if the PANEL you are considering does indeed need blending.

 1. Does the *vehicles* paint have metallic in it? (car)

2. Is the *vehicle's* paint light in color? (car)

3. Does the *panel* share a horizontal plane with a panel being refinished? (panel)

If you answer YES to the first question (metallic in the paint), then you can skip the second question and assume the vehicle qualifies for blend.

 **Cars with metallic in the paint always qualify for blend**

Metallic is the metal specks or flakes in the paint. I personally call them sparkles, but technically it is called metallic.

 **If there is NO metallic in the paint you ask the second question, "Is the vehicle light in color?"**

Except for white, all vehicles that are light in color will qualify for blend.

If the vehicle does not have metallic in the paint and is not light in color, I do not recommend applying blend on the first inspection.

The horizontal plane rule is what this guide is for. If the panel shares "the same light" or horizontal plane and there is no major gap between the panels, you should blend that panel (if it qualifies per the previous questions). As an example, you WOULD blend a quarter panel if painting the rear door on a Toyota Camry.

You would NOT blend a truck bedside panel if painting the cab on a Ford F150. The gap is TOO BIG.

Photos Guide

I've listed the standard required photos on this sheet to help make sure you NEVER miss a photo.

Use the photos guide in the lower left-hand corner to make sure you get all the required photos.

1. Left Front Corner
2. Right Front Corner
3. Right Rear Corner
4. Left Rear Corner
5. License Plate
6. VIN
7. Odometer
8. Dash
9. Headliner
10. Driver's Seat & Door
11. Carpet
12. Engine
13. Tread Depth Photos (4x)
14. Measurement Photo
15. Damage Photos (at least 3)

Repair Hours Guide

While there is no "right" repair hour number, there is an industry standard and accepted "range". This can feel overwhelming when you are just starting out. No one wants to be the new green appraiser that walks up and writes a two hours repair when it is a ten-hour dent.

To help you get a handle on what number of repairs should be, I created the IA Path "Repair Hours Guide".

I initially used this with my students from our certification course, and they found it INVALUABLE! I decided to share it within this book so you can feel the confidence they felt from not having to guess.

I break damages into 4 different categories, and all that you are left with deciding is which of these categories the damage falls into. You then use that measurement to determine how many labor hours are needed.

- **Nick** (less than 1 inch) - 0.5 hours
- **Scratch** (more than 1 inch) – 1 hour
- **Dent** – 2 hours
- **Impact** – 1 hour for how many "fists" you would need to cover the affected area of the dent

I expect that while you are looking at damages that you use your "adjuster" hat to make decisions. If a scratch is 1 hour, but you have twenty scratches on a door from an angry girlfriend keying a car… this doesn't mean twenty hours!

Use common sense to adjust accordingly. This doesn't excuse you from making a judgment call but is merely a starting point to making your decision.

Below are some examples of each type of damage. REMEMBER, the software will automatically include the refinish/paint time on the damage panels. You are just writing repair hours for fixing the damage before being painted.

Nick

This damage where the bumper and fender meet is a nick of damage on each panel. I would write .5 hours of repair time on BOTH the bumper and fender.

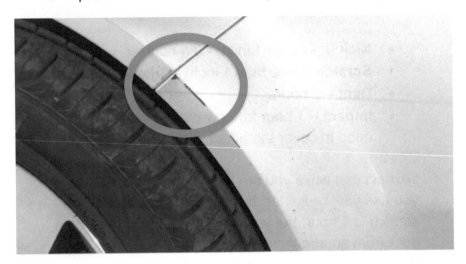

Scratch

Below is an example of the damage that would fall into the "scratch" category. I'd be writing 1 repair hour on the bumper.

Dent

This damage on the door, I'd classify as a "dent" using the IA Path Repair Hours Guide and write 2 repair hours.

Impact

While much of the damage to this vehicle obviously needs replacement, the damage to the left front door of this vehicle is NOT. I would be considering repair on this panel, and I would need to use our "impact" measurement on the IA Path Repair Hours Guide.

I'd be using my first to measure how many fists it'd take to cover the damaged area. When using this measurement, It roughly takes eight fists to cover this affected area so I'd write an eight hour repair. Some may simply replace this door, and that is an OK decision, but this is to show how to use the repair hour guide on a large dent.

Creases Cause Increases

The last thing you'll need to consider with the IA Path Repair Hours Guide is creases in the damage.

When a panel is creased, it is MORE difficult to restore back to pre-loss condition. Remember that paper airplane you made as a kid and got the crease wrong? Good luck getting it flat again... right? Metal that has been creased is VERY difficult to repair, and we'll need to think seriously about whether to replace a panel or not based on a crease.

If you decide to repair a panel that has a crease determine the number of repair hours needed based on the Repair Hours Guide and then DOUBLE it. That is how much harder it is to repair a crease.

Make sure you confirm it is cost effective to repair when compared to just replacing the panel.

Below are some examples of creases on a metal panel.

While this may only appear to be a 3-4 hours' worth of damage on this panel by our repair hours guide, I'd be doubling it due to the creases causing increases in repair time and writing 6 repair hours.

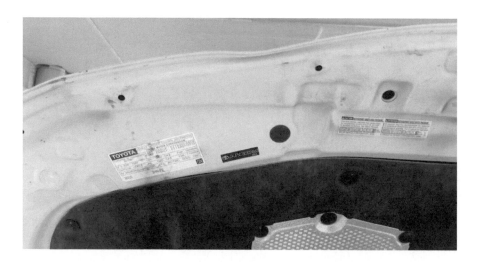

This yellow hood has a serious crease on the edge of the hood. It may only appear to be a 2-3-hour dent, but I'd be writing 6 hours to repair it. Due to the complexity of repair, it may need to be replaced, but if you'd write 6 hours repair based on the repair hour guide and remember that "creases cause increases" and double your number, you'll be in the industry acceptable repair hour range.

Part 3: The Playbook: Damages

Front End Damage

This chapter is designed to help you know the things to look for when inspecting a vehicle with front end damage.

Experienced appraisers learn after inspecting dozens of front-end hits…. They are eerily similar, and I want you to know what to look for right out of the gate.

We'll start with some general rules. Below is an example of a mild front-end hit, and following it, a major front end hit. No matter how severe the damage or how light, I recommend following these guidelines of what to look for.

Inspect from the Front Back

When inspecting a vehicle with lots of damage, you can forget what you have written down on your scope notes, or added to your estimating system, if you aren't systematic in your approach.

Try to write damage down by starting with the front bumper cover and moving backwards. Below is an example of what major parts I'm going to confirm damage on, in order (while also keeping my eye out for less obvious items to photograph and add).

1. Front Bumper
   a. Cover
   b. Absorber
   c. Reinforcement
2. Grille
3. Headlights
4. Cooling
   a. Condenser
   b. Radiator
   c. Reservoirs
5. Radiator Support
6. Inner Structure
   a. Frame Rails
   b. Inner Fender
7. Hood
8. Fenders

Open the Hood

It may seem obvious, but at times, some IA's don't take the time or give the effort to open a hood. Even on a small hit, it can be revealing of how extensive (or not) the damage is to the front of the vehicle, if you simply open the hood.

This also makes it easier to look for damages to many of the parts I listed above. Taking photos of the inside of the engine compartment with the hood up, even if no damage exists, helps the insurance company feel as if they got the whole picture of the damages the vehicle sustained.

Check the Headlight Tabs

It is common on front end collisions that damage to the headlights exist, yet it isn't always obvious.

Be sure to check the bottom of the headlight and the head light tabs where the headlight are bolted to the vehicle. These often crack during impact and are not always obvious until you look closely.

Move the headlight around with your hand and see if it moves. This can save an obvious supplement item from popping up in the future.

Look for Cooling Damage

The condenser is directly behind the bumper reinforcement and gets damaged when the reinforcement is pushed back into it.

Both the condenser and radiator are very fragile and are commonly damaged. Look for leaking fluid, other parts stuck into them, and look for cracks at the top of the condenser and radiator where they bolt into the radiator support.

The collision can cause cracks in the tabs and housing, but you must look to see this damage.

Also take a quick look at both the windshield washer and coolant reservoir. Try to move them with your hand. Put your hand on it and look at it from above and below if possible.

Is There Frame Damage?

Does the front end look shoved one way or another? Is it all pushed backward? If you feel it is, you are probably right.

There is likely frame damage that needs repaired or at least re-alignment of the sheet metal is needed.

If things look off, add two hours of set up and measure to confirm. If you are certain the frame has damage add two hours Pull for either Sidesway or Mash. See the chapter on frame damage for further explanation.

Rear End Damage

This chapter is designed to help you walkthrough the things to look for when inspecting a vehicle with rear end damage.

Experienced appraisers learn after inspecting dozens of rear-end hits…. They can be very similar, and I want you to know what to look for right out of the gate.

We'll start with some general rules. Below is an example of a mild rear end hit and a major rear end hit. No matter how severe the damage, or how light the damage is, I recommend following these guidelines of what to look for.

Inspect from the Back to the Front

Here we may break a few of my own rules and guidelines. I typically tell you to inspect from the front to the back, BUT when inspecting a rear end hit it can be easier to document and understand if you start from the rear and make your way forward.

Try to write damage down, starting with the rear bumper cover and moving forward. Below is an example of what major parts I'm going to confirm damage on, in order (while also keeping my eye out for less obvious items to photograph and add).

1. Rear Bumper
   a. Cover
   b. Absorber
   c. Reinforcement
2. Rear Lamps
3. Tailgate/Trunk
4. Muffler
5. Rear Body Panel
6. Rear Floor Pan
7. Package Tray (Holds Spare Tire)
8. Inner Structure
   a. Rear Frame Rails
   b. Inner Quarter Panels/Wheelhouse
9. Quarter Panels
10. Uniside

Open the Liftgate/Trunk/Tailgate

It may seem obvious, but at times some IA's don't take the time or effort to open a hood. Even on a small hit, it can be revealing of how extensive (or not) the damage is to the front of the vehicle, if you simply open the trunk and pull the carpet back.

This also makes it easier to look for damages to many of the parts I listed above. Taking photos of the inside of the rear floor pan and spare tire compartment with the trunk up, even if no damage exists, helps the insurance company feel as if they got the whole picture of the damages the vehicle sustained.

Check the Rear Body Panel

I've gotten push back on this rule from a few IA's, because they envisioned a job where they didn't have to get dirty or get on the ground…. Well I'm here to tell you, sometimes you need to get dirty.

Get on the ground and get underneath the rear of the vehicle and look at the rear body panel. This is a very expensive item to replace and gets damaged frequently. Also, double check the rear floor pan while you are down there.

 Carry a tarp with you in your vehicle. Use this to save your clothes from getting dirty while needing to inspect underneath the car.

Look for Frame Damage

The sneakiest of damages that happen to a vehicle is frame damage at the rear of the vehicle. With a spare tire hanging down and a muffler in the way it can be hard to spot damages to the rear frame rail, if the damage is not extremely obvious.

One thing to check on rear end collision vehicles is the quarter panels and unisides. When a frame gives from a rear end collision, the rear sheet metal (Quarter panel and uniside), must also give somewhere. This can cause a small circle or indention in either the quarter panel or the start of the roof rail/sail panel where the uniside transitions from the quarter to the roof rail.

Double check for dimples or indentions. See my example below of a mild looking hit that ended up with BIG frame damage.

I doubt you'd miss this quarter panel damage, but it's a great (but extreme) example of how a small rear end hit can cause big frame damage and cause the quarter panel/uniside to buckle.

Rear View

Side View

If you see a small indention or believe that there is frame damage add "Set Up and Measure" for 2hrs and a "Rear Frame Pull for Mash/Sidesway" for 2hrs. If you need more help with frame damage, see the chapter dedicated to it.

Side or T-Bone Damage

This chapter will guide you through a few different things to consider or look at when dealing with a side impact, sideswipe, or T-bone collision.

There isn't as much damage hiding on a T-bone collision as a front or rear end collision, but knowing what to expect and look for can save you time and mental bandwidth.

The Uniside

When a T-bone collision happens, the first thing you are going to really look for, other than obvious damages, is damage to the uniside.

The uniside is from the windshield pillar all the way back to the quarter panel, down to the rocker, and at the top is the roof rail above the doors. I call it the "frame" of the side of the vehicle and it is frequently damaged from heavy side impacts.

Pillar Damage

Look for damage near the pillars, if possible open up the doors, and if the doors are stuck shut, climb in from the other side and look from the inside.

Pillar damage is hard to repair, so I'd recommend determining your repair hours and then doubling it.

Rocker Panel

Get down on the ground, if needed, and see if the rocker panel has suffered damages. Once again, if possible, open the doors and inspect the bottom of the uniside, AKA the rocker panel.

This is tough to repair as well, so double any repair hour guesses you may have when starting out.

Unibody Pull

When the front or rear of vehicle suffers frame damage, we write for set up and measure, and time to pull the frame. When the "side frame" suffers damage, it is similar.

If there is uniside damage, put 2hrs for Set Up and Measure and 2hrs for Unibody Pull. This will give the shop time to measure how far off the side of the vehicle is and then time to use a frame machine to pull it back into proper alignment.

Floor Pan

The floor of the vehicle is called the "Floor Pan". It can be hard to determine if there are damages to the floor pan just by staring at the side of the vehicle.
Get on the ground and look to see if anything looks damaged or kinked. Also, try pulling up the carpet on the side of the impact and look for damages. Another trick is to just feel the floor through the carpet and see if you can feel any damages.

Insurance companies normally won't let you write damages you can't see, but knowing that the floor pan is damaged can help you determine what pictures you need to justify this major repair item.

Interior Trim

The interior of the vehicle can get forgotten when we are distracted with twisted metal on the outside, but there are often broken interior pieces from side collisions.

Interior door trim panels, pillar trim, carpet, headliner, or even the dash can sustain damage, and if you aren't looking for it, you'll likely miss the damages.

Tire or Rim Damage

Sideswipes and T-bones often result in impacts to the wheels and tires of the vehicle. Be sure to inspect each tire on the side of the impact AND on the opposite side for damages.

I've seen a lot of collisions where the impact pushed the vehicle into a curb or another object on the non-damaged side which resulted in broken rims and a needed alignment.

If you see damage from an impact to the tire or rim, replace the item damaged, an alignment ($69.99 for 2-wheel alignment, $89.99 for 4-wheel), and mount and balance for $15.

Cooling Damage

A real quick blitz on some of the parts of the coolant system. These all are damaged frequently in front collisions.

Radiator

The radiator is responsible for the cooling of the engine. This is usually located behind the condenser and in front of the radiator support.

Condenser

The condenser is responsible for your air conditioner. This is usually located in front of the radiator.

Trans-Cooler

It appears like a mini version of the radiator or condenser and is typically in front of both of them. This guy helps cool down the transmission.

Cooling Fan Assembly

Usually located behind the radiator, the cooling fan assembly helps the air flow through the radiator and condenser.

Coolant Reservoir

The coolant reservoir is where the radiator's reserve of coolant is located. In a collision, this plastic container is easily broken.

Windshield Washer Fluid Reservoir

The windshield washer fluid reservoir holds the fluid for the windshield washer fluid. It too is easily broken, being made of plastic. It can be many different shapes and sizes.

When to Replace a Cooling Part

Great news is, if there is any damage to any of the parts listed, you simply replace the part.

No attempting repair or anything like that, when in doubt throw it out.

Most insurance companies will allow you to use aftermarket cooling parts, but as always check your guidelines.

Additional Operations

When replacing a condenser and/or radiator, there are a few additional operations you'll want to add onto your estimate.

Audatex will ask you if you want to add some of these operations, and CCC One has these operations under the additional operations of the corresponding section.

Radiator Replaced

Replace Economy/Aftermarket – Coolant - $20

Condenser Replaced

A/C Evac, Recharge, & Recovery – 3.0hrs (use built in system time)

This is telling the repair facility to make sure the air conditioning lines get all the freon removed, then recharge it and save as much as possible.

Frame Damage

One of the most common fears I hear from my students is,

"I don't know what to write about frame damage."

I get their concern. This was one of my major concerns for a long time. As an adjuster or appraiser, you are constantly feeling like you don't know EVERYTHING about a vehicle or the repair process, because we only see what vehicles look like pre-repair, and if we re-inspect for a supplement, it is but a brief glance at a repair in process.

This feeling can be enhanced by shops who at times can be insulting and say off the wall comments like, "Why did you write such a bad estimate?" or "The original estimate on this was crap."

Now, forgive the shop, because they, like us, often forget we have a different role from them.

They are the repair experts, we are "estimating" only what we can see. Our job isn't to nail an estimate from the beginning, our job is to tell a story about what we can see about the vehicle as it sits in its current state.
Why do I go to such lengths to talk about this? Because it is imperative that you know what your job is. I need you thinking about writing what you can see, not what a shop will find after a tear down.

Frame Damage Repair

I will help you get the thirty-thousand-foot view of frame damage repair, only because if you understand it, you'll remember my best practices better.

To determine if a vehicle has damage to the frame, shops **set up** the vehicle on a **frame machine,** and then **measure** the vehicle, comparing it to what the manufacturer says the vehicle should be.

This tells them, for 100% certainty, if the frame is damaged and in what direction.

What I just described above, we write as a repair operation called, **"Set Up and Measure"**.

Whenever possible frame damage exists, write an estimate line for "Set up and Measure" for 2hrs. Change the labor rate category to "frame".

Once damage is documented, they then hook the vehicle to the frame machine, with thick chains and hooks, and slowly **pull** the vehicle's frame back into proper alignment.

As I said, big overview of what they do. Depending on the type of frame damage that exists will determine what type of "pulling" they do.

The pulling is typically listed as "Pull for _____ (fill in the blank with the type of frame damage)."

The major different types of frame damage I use are listed below. There are a few others, but if you know these, you'll know what to do when the time comes.

- **Pull for Mash** – Front or rear end collision, frame is pushed back on itself… think accordion.
- **Pull for Sidesway** – the front or rear of the vehicle is off to the side more than it should be.
- **Pull Unibody** – This is when damage exists to the uniside from a heavy side impact like a T-bone.

When writing for any of the above frame pulls on an original estimate, I estimate two hours repair for the shop to perform those operations.

 When writing for any type of frame pull, use the descriptions I used listed above and write 2hrs repair. Don't forget to change the labor rate to "frame".

This will get you in the ballpark of what is needed for the vehicle. The shop, IA Firm, and insurance company will know that you recognize frame damage likely exists, and it will not be a shock when additional time is requested by the shop on a supplement.

Air Bag Deployed

In our industry, everything regarding safety, computers, and electronics is getting increasingly complicated.

It can be hard to keep up with the manufacturer's guidelines for repairing the vehicle, but the good news is that when an air bag is deployed, there is a standard written out inside of our estimating systems that tells us EXACTLY what needs to be added to our estimate based on which air bag was deployed inside of the vehicle.

Before we get to the specific operations and line items that need to be added, let's first cover the main air bags that modern vehicles are equipped with.

Steering Wheel/Driver's Air Bag

Inside of every steering wheel is an air bag. This is one of the most common air bags that are deployed in a collision.

It is there to keep the driver's head from hitting the steering wheel.

Instrument Panel/Passenger's Air Bag

In front of the passenger is an air bag very similar to the air bag that is inside the steering wheel.

This air bag is only deployed when the vehicle's sensors detect someone is sitting in the passenger's seat.

Like the steering wheel air bag, this is designed to keep the passenger from hitting the dash.

Roof/Curtain Air Bags

Along the interior of the roof, on both sides of the vehicle, is a large air bag that is called a curtain air bag.

This air bag is there to keep an occupant's head from hitting the side of the vehicle in a collision.

Seat Air Bags

These air bags are built into the side of the seats and deploy to help the passenger's body from hitting the side of the vehicle.

Now that we know the common air bags, let's talk about a few of the other major safety items related to air bags that we must be familiar with to be able to properly write an estimate where an air bag is deployed.

Air Bag Control Module

All of the air bags listed above are controlled by an onboard computer called the air bag module.

This ultra-control panel is VITAL to the safety of all the occupants trusting the vehicle to help keep them safe in the event of a collision.

Sensors

The control module listed above is getting information from sensors that are located all over the exterior of the vehicle. Some of the common sensors are:

- Front Bumper Sensors
- Door Sensors
- Quarter Sensors
- Rear Bumper Sensors

As mentioned before, there are also sensors in the seats that inform the control module whether a seat has an occupant in the vehicle or not.

Seat Belts

Seat belts play a major role in assisting the air bags with their job of keeping the occupant safe.
There is a seat belt located at every seat of the vehicle.

 Check all seat belts during your inspection. If a seat belt is "limp" or stays extended, it needs replaced. Also, If an air bag was deployed for that seat, replace the corresponding seat belt.

Common Practice: Estimate Items After an Air Bag Deployment

Inside of the estimating systems, under the air bags and safety section, you'll find a detailed explanation of what to replace when an air bag is deployed.

USE THAT AS YOUR ESTIMATING BIBLE! BELOW IS A LIST OF COMMON THINGS THAT ARE UNIVERSAL BUT NOT VEHICLE SPECIFIC!

Steering Wheel/Driver's Air Bag Deployed

When a steering wheel is deployed, there are a few items that I know from repetition that I'll need to replace. AGAIN, check the estimating system for the manufacturer's guidelines for an air bag deployment to see the exact items for the vehicle you are writing an estimate for.

- R&R Steering Wheel Air Bag
- Air Bag Control Module
- Clock spring (Part of the Steering Wheel)
- Driver's Seat Belt (Buckle & Retainer)
- Sensors Near Impact

Instrument Panel/Passenger's Air Bag Deployed

When an instrument panel air bag is deployed, there are a few items that I know from repetition that I'll need to replace. AGAIN, check the estimating system for the manufacturer's guidelines for an air bag deployment to see the exact items for the vehicle you are writing an estimate for.

- Instrument Panel Air Bag
- Air Bag Control Module
- Passenger's Seat Belt
- Sensors Near Impact

Roof/Curtain Air Bag Deployed

When a roof air bag is deployed, there are a few items that I know from repetition that I'll need to replace. AGAIN, check the estimating system for the manufacturer's guidelines for an air bag deployment to see the exact items for the vehicle you are writing an estimate for.

- Curtain Air Bag
- Air Bag Control Module
- Seat Belts That Were in Use
- Headliner (rips from air bag deployment)
- Sensors Near Impact

Seat Air Bag Deployed

When a seat air bag is deployed, there are a few items that I know from repetition that I'll need to replace. AGAIN, check the estimating system for the manufacturer's guidelines for an air bag deployment to see the exact items for the vehicle you are writing an estimate for.

- Seat Air Bag
- Air Bag Control Module
- Seat Belts Associated
- Seat Cover (rips from air bag deployment)
- Sensors Near Impact

Glass Damage

Broken glass happens a lot more than you might think and is straightforward to deal with, but there are some things you should know.

Replacement Glass Part Types

I have NEVER used LKQ/Used glass when writing an estimate.

Now, this isn't because I couldn't or don't recommend it, but early on I learned shops didn't like dealing with LKQ glass. No one knows if the glass you found has a nick in it, is pitted up, etc.

There are normally three options when replacing glass.

- OEM
- NAGS

- Sublet Repair

Both the OEM and NAGS pricing are normally built into the estimating software, but sublet repair is not.

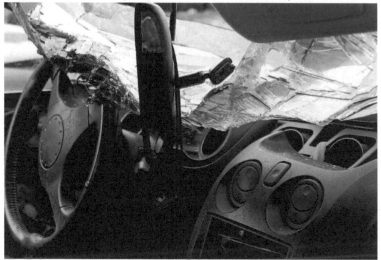

Sublet Repair Glass or Safelite Glass

It is VERY common that you are required to get a quote from Safelite auto glass on all glass replacement items.

This isn't hard or very time consuming, just more of a mental nuisance than anything.

1. **Go to Google and type in Safelite Glass Quote**
2. **Find the Correct Site and Choose That You are an Insurance Company**
3. **Input the Vehicle & Glass Information**

4. Finish the Form to Get the Quote

This process can be done in two minutes, and on a repairable vehicle, will prove that you know how to follow guidelines. On total loss vehicles I rarely get a Safelite Quote.

OEM and NAGS are only a good option if cost effective. Cost effectiveness is always king, after guidelines to an insurance company.

 TIP *Add a glass kit for each glass you are replacing. Standard pricing is $15 - $20 per kit.*

Flood Damage

This chapter will help you if you are dealing with vehicles that have suffered a saltwater flood, freshwater flood, brackish (combo of salt and fresh) water flood, or even the common scenario of a vehicle driving through a deep puddle then stalls.

Flood vehicles can present interesting challenges to you as an IA. It is likely that a vehicle will be a total loss if submerged in water, but as appraisers and adjusters, we can't simply "total loss" a car. We must prove what is damaged and make a compelling case for making a vehicle go away.

The key is knowing what to look for and documenting what the damage is. Even if you can't total loss the vehicle, properly documenting on an original inspection can help you with any supplements in the future.

Engine Damage

I always hated trying to figure out if a vehicle had engine damage from a flood. It stressed me out, I've never been a mechanic, and I felt incompetent to make that determination.

Good news is I talked with different experts in the industry and created a best practice, so whether you are a mechanic or not can determine if an engine has damage from a flood... or not.

- **Check for milky oil** (if milky replace engine)
- **Check for water in the air intake**
- **If water is present, try starting the engine**
- **If it acts "locked" or won't turn over, replace the engine**

Take good photos documenting the milky oil. You'll want to show that the oil doesn't look black or a beautiful rich gold color. If it is milky, it will look more like chocolate milk.

For the air intake, take a photo of the air filter itself. Is it wet? Are there water droplets inside the airbox? If so, this typically causes a hydro-locked engine.

 Purchase a small screwdriver and socket set to keep in your car. You may need it to be able to open air filter boxes.

A hydro-locked engine occurs when an engine suffers damage from the force of the pistons moving upward, causing a connecting rod to bend, a crack in the crankshaft, or fractures in the cylinder walls. It can also blow out the oil seals, which allows water to get into the oil (thus the milky water).

I've seen broken rods break through an engine block, and according to IA's who handle WAY more flood than me, 90% of all vehicles that have a flood loss description (whether driving through a big puddle or not) end up being total losses once it arrives at the shop.

The biggest mistake IA's make is not documenting the milky oil or water in the air intake.

Flood Levels

You'll hear talk of what level was the water in the car. Flood levels is a scale that is commonly used to indicate how submerged a vehicle was in the water.

There are typically four flood levels that tell what the highest point that the water reached was,

- **Level 1** – Up to the Rocker Panel (not inside the vehicle)
- **Level 2** – Inside the Vehicle (on the floor)
- **Level 3** – Up to the Seats

- **Level 4** – To the Dash

You can probably figure out on your own from this scale that determining how high the water got on the vehicle is a TOP priority with flooded vehicles.

 If a vehicle suffered a freshwater level 3 and beyond, ALWAYS recommend a total loss.

 If the vehicle suffered a saltwater or brackish level 2 and beyond, ALWAYS recommend a total loss

Water Lines

As discussed in other parts of this book, our job as auto damage appraisers and adjusters is to DOCUMENT THE DAMAGE. Showing in a photograph how high the water was is mission critical on a flood vehicle.

If this vehicle drove through a large puddle and sucked up water into the engine, it may not have a water line, but in most cases, it will.

You'll be looking for a line of dirt or debris on the vehicle. See the example below for an easy example of a flood line during Hurricane Sandy.

If the vehicle you are inspecting is NOT this obvious of a flood line, look at the door jambs. Many times, this will give you a good indication of how high the water was.

Showing where the water reached on the vehicle is important because water does crazy things to a vehicle.

1. **It can ruin electrical components and connectors**
2. **Mold and mildew the interior**
3. **Create a biohazard from the dirty water**
4. **Cause safety systems to fail**

Flood Template

Below is a flood template I created during Hurricane Harvey. The flood template makes it easy for you to use as a scope sheet during your flood loss. Select how high the water level was, and ALWAYS document the option of the vehicle to make sure you can properly complete a valuation form and the total loss process.

PATH

Owner_____ Vehicle _____ Mileage _____

Vin __ __ __ __ __ __ __ __ __ __ __ __ __ __ __ __ __   Color _____

Transmission	☐ Automatic	☐ S6	☐ S5	☐ S4	☐ S3	☐ OD	☐ 4W	☐ PO

Power Options
- ☐ PS Power Steering
- ☐ PB Power Brakes
- ☐ PW Power Windows
- ☐ PL Power Locks
- ☐ SP Power Driver Seat
- ☐ PC Power Passenger Seat
- ☐ PA Power Antenna
- ☐ PM Power Mirrors
- ☐ PT Power Trunk/Tailgate
- ☐ PP Power Adjustable Pedals
- ☐ PD Power Sliding Door
- ☐ DP Dual Power Sliding Doors

Décor/Convenience
- ☐ AC Air Conditioning
- ☐ DA Dual Air Conditioning
- ☐ CL Climate Control
- ☐ RD Rear Defogger
- ☐ IW Intermittent Wipers
- ☐ TW Tilt Wheel
- ☐ TL Telescopic Wheel
- ☐ CC Cruise Control
- ☐ KE Keyless Entry
- ☐ CN Console/Storage
- ☐ CO Overhead Console
- ☐ EC Entertainment Center
- ☐ NV Navigation System
- ☐ C2 Communications System
- ☐ HU Heads Up Display
- ☐ WT Wood Interior Trim
- ☐ EI Electronic Instrumentation
- ☐ IB On Board Computer
- ☐ MC Message Center
- ☐ MM Memory Package
- ☐ RJ Remote Start

Seating
- ☐ CS Cloth Seats
- ☐ LS Leather Seats
- ☐ RL Reclining/ Lounge Seats
- ☐ BS Bucket Seats
- ☐ SH Heated Seats (2)
- ☐ RH Rear Heated Seats
- ☐ 3S Third Row Seat
- ☐ 3P Power Third Seat
- ☐ RJ Retractable Seats
- ☐ 2P 12 Passenger Seating
- ☐ 5P 15 Passenger Seating
- ☐ B2 Captain Chairs (2)
- ☐ B4 Captain Chairs (4)
- ☐ B6 Captain Chairs (6)

Radio
- ☐ AM AM Radio
- ☐ FM FM Radio
- ☐ ST Stereo
- ☐ CA Cassette
- ☐ SE Search/Seek
- ☐ CD Compact Disc Player
- ☐ SK CD Changer/Stacker
- ☐ UR Premium Radio
- ☐ XM Satellite Radio
- ☐ TQ Steering Wheel Touch

Controls
- ☐ M3 Auxiliary Audio Connection
- ☐ EQ Equalizer
- ☐ CB CB Radio
- ☐ 8T 8 Track Tape Player

Wheels
- ☐ AW Aluminum/Alloy Wheels
- ☐ CJ Chrome Wheels
- ☐ W2 20" or Larger Wheels
- ☐ DC Deluxe Wheel Covers
- ☐ FC Full Wheel Covers
- ☐ SA Spoke Aluminum Wheels
- ☐ SY Styled Steel Wheels
- ☐ WW Wire Wheels
- ☐ WC Wire Wheel Covers
- ☐ RW Rally Wheels
- ☐ KW Locking Wheels
- ☐ LC Locking Wheel Covers

Roof
- ☐ EG Electric Glass Roof
- ☐ ES Electric Steel Roof
- ☐ OR Skyview Roof
- ☐ SD Dual Power Roofs
- ☐ MS Manual Steel Roof
- ☐ MG Manual Glass Roof
- ☐ FR Flip Roof
- ☐ TT T-Top Panel
- ☐ GT Glass T-Top/Panel
- ☐ MV Manual Convertible Roof
- ☐ VP Power Convertible Roof
- ☐ RM Detachable Roof
- ☐ VR Vinyl Roof
- ☐ RF Cabriolet Roof
- ☐ LR Landau Roof
- ☐ LP Padded Landau Roof
- ☐ PV Padded Vinyl Roof
- ☐ CT Soft Top
- ☐ HT Hard Top

Safety/Brakes
- ☐ AG Air Bag
- ☐ RG Passenger Air Bag
- ☐ XG Front Side Impact Air Bags
- ☐ ZG Rear Side Impact Air Bags
- ☐ DG Head/Roof Air Bags
- ☐ TD Theft Deterrent Alarm
- ☐ VZ Night Vision
- ☐ IC Intelligent Cruise
- ☐ PJ Parking Sensors
- ☐ PX Parking Sensors W/Equip
- ☐ AB Anti-Lock Brakes (4)
- ☐ A2 Anti-Lock Brakes (2)
- ☐ DB 4-Wheel Disc Brakes
- ☐ RB Rollover Protection
- ☐ TX Traction Control
- ☐ T1 Stability Control
- ☐ AL Auto Level

Exterior/Paint/Glass
- ☐ RR Luggage/Roof Rack
- ☐ WG Woodgrain
- ☐ WP Rear Window Wiper
- ☐ 2T Two Tone Paint
- ☐ D2 Deluxe 2 Tone Paint
- ☐ HP Three Stage Paint
- ☐ IP Clearcoat Paint
- ☐ MP Metallic Paint
- ☐ SL Rear Spoiler
- ☐ FL Fog Lamps
- ☐ TG Tinted Glass
- ☐ DT Privacy Glass
- ☐ BN Body Side Moldings
- ☐ DM Dual Mirrors
- ☐ HM Heated Mirrors
- ☐ HV Headlamp Washers
- ☐ MX Signal Integrated Mirrors

Other
- ☐ BD Running Board/Side Steps
- ☐ UP Power Retractable Running Boards
- ☐ XE Xenon Headlamps
- ☐ AR Bed Rails
- ☐ BL Bedliner
- ☐ BY Bedliner (Spray On)
- ☐ CP Fiberglass Cap
- ☐ GG Grill Guard
- ☐ SB Rear Step Bumper
- ☐ SS Swivel Seats
- ☐ SW Rear Sliding Window
- ☐ PG Power Rear Window
- ☐ TB Tool Box (Permanent)
- ☐ TN Tonneau Cover – Soft
- ☐ TZ Tonneau Cover – Hard
- ☐ TP Trailering Package
- ☐ WD Dual Rear Wheels
- ☐ XT Auxiliary Fuel Tank
- ☐ 3D 3rd Truck Door
- ☐ 4D 4th Door Truck/Van
- ☐ BC Bumper Cushions
- ☐ BG Bumper Guards
- ☐ EM California Emissions
- ☐ SG Stone Guard
- ☐ WI Winch

☐ Below AVG

☐ Average

☐ Above Average

☐ Milky Oil

☐ Water in Air Filter

☐ Saltwater   ☐ Brackish   ☐ Freshwater

(1) Rocker (2) To Floor (3) To Seat (4) To Dash

(Not in Car)

Common Operations Per Flood Level

During hurricane Harvey and Irma, I looked at more than ten guidelines from insurance companies and IA Firms as to what they wanted to be performed on the different flood levels to determine a best practice for you as an IA.

You may be instructed to write different items, and that is OK, but this will help you write a good initial estimate and will make you look like you are a seasoned flood appraiser.

Always follow your company guidelines, if you are not given specific operations, **this is a general guide for you to use.**

Level 1 - Rocker Panel (Not in Vehicle)

- **Oil Change/Service - Sublet $35.00**
- **Transmission Service - Sublet $150**
- **Check Air Filter - Sublet $35**
- **Clean/Lube Brakes - Sublet $100**
- **Clean CV Joints - Sublet $75**
- **Re-Pack Bearings - Sublet $300 (optional)**
- **Axle Service - Sublet $100**
- **Dry Electrical Parts- Sublet $225**
- **Clean Exterior - Sublet $70**

Level 2 - Floor (in Vehicle)

- **Everything in Level 1 +**
- **Clean/Dry Carpet - Sublet $325**
- **Clean Seat Belts - Sublet $35**
- **Clean Trim- Sublet $95**
- **Disinfect Interior - Sublet $75**
- **Check Control Mods - Sublet $75**

Level 3 – Seats

Many companies Total Vehicles Once Flood Reaches
Level 3

- **Everything in Level 1 & 2 +**
- **Seat Covers - Sublet $120**
- **Clean Seats - Sublet $100**
- **Dry Door Panels - Sublet $120**
- **Lube Seat Tracks- Sublet $35**
- **Lube Window Tracks - Sublet $35**

Level 4 – Dash

A Vehicle Will ALWAYS Be a Total Loss Once Flood
Reaches Level 4

- **Everything in Level 1, 2, & 3+**

- Flood Level 4 - Sublet $0.01
- OBVIOUS TOTAL LOSS - Sublet $0.01

Hail Damage

I want to give you a basic understanding of how to determine the damage that the hail has caused to an owner's vehicle. Once you look at and touch hail dents, this chapter will make a lot more sense than it does as words on a page, but you need to know these basics to be armed and ready to jump right into being a hail adjuster.

There are a few simple techniques and things to look for that will greatly enhance your accuracy of estimating. Many veteran adjusters are not even aware of these tips. You will be ready to succeed if you understand and use the following techniques I am going to lay out in this chapter. Don't be afraid to reference back to this chapter and book as a reference manual.

Light Bending

This adjusting superpower will give you x-ray-like vision to see hail dents that average adjusters and owners cannot see. There are many misconceptions on how to properly look at a vehicle, but this is the technique of true professionals.

I want you to do an exercise the next time you are outside with your vehicle. Look at your hood and find reflections in your hood. Do you see the clouds? How about the light pole? Telephone or power wires? The old barn? Whatever you see in your reflection off the hood, focus on one object. Now move your head and keep track of your object. Walk to the left, now to the right. Were you able to keep the reflection the whole time? Good.

Now, I want you to find a hardline in the reflection. This is a light pole, edge of a roof, anything that is solid and a different color than its surroundings. Your goal, each and every time you look at a hail damaged panel, is to find a hardline reflection. Find one that is straight and stands out in the reflection.

When you move your head and the hardline comes across a hail dent, you will see your light bending superpower in action. The hardline reflection will bend to the shape of the hail dent. It will become distorted and reveal how far the metal has been stretched. This is because the metal is not flat at this spot.

That is how you find dents and properly size the dents. When looking at a dent on a hood what you can see with your naked eye is only part of the stretched metal. When you use your light bending powers, you will see the true size of the dent.

This same technique is extremely useful in counting the dents across a panel. Each time you see the reflection flicker or go distorted, you know a hail dent is present.

PDR
Now that you know how to find the dents, how are you supposed to know if a dent can be fixed? The primary and preferred way a hail dent is repaired is a process known as paintless dent repair, or for short, PDR.

PDR is the process by which a technician massages the hail dent from the backside of a panel. If a PDR technician cannot get access underneath the dent, they will try to pull up on the dent using a technique called glue pulling.

Understanding the method of which the repairs are done is a critical piece in learning how to identify the types of repair that will be needed to repair a hail dent.

Sheet metal has a memory, and because of that memory, it wants to go flat again. If a technician pushes a dent past the flat spot they have a tool to tap the dent down again. The repair of hail is a very tedious process as the technician fixes each dent individually, across the entire vehicle.

PDR/Hail Matrix

A PDR matrix is a chart used to determine the cost needed to pay a PDR technician for the damage on a panel. Most PDR matrices are agreed upon by insurance companies as the standard by which the price is determined.

Using a PDR matrix is as easy as 1, 2, 3.

1. You must first determine what panel you are assessing the damage on. Find the panel in the left column of the chart.
2. Next, determine how many dents you found on that panel of the vehicle.
3. Lastly, decide what size the dents are. There are 4 sizes to choose from: dime, nickel, quarter, and half dollar.

Hail, by its very nature, is random, and the sizes of dents can vary across the panel. It's up to you as the adjuster to make a decision of what size the *majority of the dents are.*

If there are 16 dents total, 5 being quarters, 5 being dime, and 6 being nickel, the panel then has 16 nickel size dents.

Once you know the average size of the dent you can then determine the dollar amount. Using the PDR/Hail Pricing Matrix, you can determine the price associated with that panel, with that dent count, and that dent size. See the image below to see a PDR/Hail pricing matrix.

PDR Price Matrix
Easy as 1,2,3
Determine
1. Panel 2. Count 3. Size

SEVERITY CLASS TOTAL # DENTS	VERY LIGHT 1 TO 5 DENTS				LIGHT 6 TO 15 DENTS				MODERATE 16 TO 30 DENTS				MEDIUM 31 TO 50 DENTS				ADD
AVERAGE SIZE	DIME	NKL	QTR	HALF	DIME	NKL	QTR	HALF	DIME	NKL	QTR	HALF	DIME	NKL	QTR	HALF	R & I
Hood	75	100	125	150	125	150	175	225	175	200	225	300	275	325	375	450	Hood/Liner
Roof	100	125	150	200	175	200	225	250	250	275	325	375	350	400	475	525	Headliner/Sunroof
Deck Lid	75	75	100	125	100	125	175	200	150	175	225	250	200	250	300	350	Trunk & Liner
Rt Roof Rail	75	100	100	125	100	125	150	175	150	200	CR	CR	200	225	CR	CR	
Lt Roof Rail	75	100	100	125	100	125	150	175	150	200	CR	CR	200	225	CR	CR	
L Quarter	75	75	100	125	100	125	150	175	150	200	225	CR	200	225	275	CR	Tail Light
LR Door	75	75	100	125	100	125	150	175	150	200	225	CR	200	225	CR	CR	Door Liner
LF Door	75	75	100	125	100	125	150	175	150	200	225	CR	200	225	CR	CR	Door Liner
L Fender	75	75	100	125	100	125	150	175	150	200	225	CR	200	225	CR	CR	Light & F Liner
R Fender	75	75	100	125	100	125	150	175	150	200	225	CR	200	225	CR	CR	Light & F Liner
RF Door	75	75	100	125	100	125	150	175	150	200	225	CR	200	225	CR	CR	Door Liner
RR Door	75	75	100	125	100	125	150	175	150	200	225	CR	200	225	CR	CR	Door Liner
R Quarter	75	75	100	125	100	125	150	175	150	200	225	CR	200	225	275	CR	Tail Light
Metal Sunroof	75	75	100	125	100	125	150	175	150	200	CR	CR	200	CR	CR	CR	Sunroof
Cowl, Other	75	75	100	125	100	125	150	175	150	200	CR	CR	200	CR	CR	CR	Cowl, Etc

SEVERITY CLASS TOTAL # DENTS	HEAVY 51 TO 75 DENTS				SEVERE 76 TO 100 DENTS				EXTREME 101 TO 150 DENTS				LIMIT 151 TO 200 DENTS				CEILING 201 TO 250 DENTS			
AVERAGE SIZE	DIME	NKL	QTR	HALF	DIME	NKL	QTR	HALF	DIME	NKL	QTR	HALF	DIME	NKL	QTR	HALF	DIME	NKL	QTR	HALF
Hood	325	350	450	575	375	450	550	650	450	600	CR	CR	575	675	CR	CR	675	775	CR	CR
Roof	425	500	625	725	450	525	675	850	525	600	700	950	675	800	975	1300	800	975	1200	1400
Deck Lid	350	400	450	550	375	450	575	CR	450	575	CR	CR	600	CR	CR	CR	700	CR	CR	CR

When writing for PDR, there are a few markups you need to consider. Markups are additional costs associated with the repair due to the level of difficulty involved.

If a panel is aluminum or high strength steel, you will add a 25% markup to the sublet repair price you determined using the PDR/Hail Matrix. To do this math quickly with a calculator, input the sublet repair price and multiply it by 1.25 to get the total price, including the markup.

Example
$100 x 1.25 = $125 with markup.

There are two other types of markups. First, there is a 25% markup for double metal. The main panel that this is used on is for the roof rails of the vehicle. Every roof rail has double metal and the PDR technician cannot access the backside of the panel. Lastly, there is a 25% markup for SUV, van, and extended cab truck roofs. If a truck has 4 full doors, then it gets a 25% markup.

Any dent that is larger than a half dollar is considered an oversize dent. Add $40 per oversize dent (check your guidelines) on the panels sublet repair price. This is added after any markup and is **usually put into your estimating system as a separate line item**.

Now that we have established how to get a price of a PDR only panel, let's explore a few things to look for to see if a panel can be repaired with just PDR.

Cone vs. Cavern
There are a few tips to help you determine if a dent can be repaired or not. This is not a perfect science, so you will always be learning.

I mentioned that metal has a memory, but there is a point where the metal is stretched far enough that it doesn't retain the memory and cannot be fixed using PDR. To identify if a dent has been stretched too far, I use my fingers to feel the dent.

Most hail dents have a cone shape. The dent starts out wide and gets skinnier as it goes down into the metal. Let's do an exercise to help you visualize what I'm saying.

Put your hand out flat with the palm up. Now take your index finger from your other hand and push down on your palm, cupping your hand as the finger hits the palm. The finger represents hail and your palm represents a metal panel on your vehicle. Do you see how your hand is at its widest at the surface and as you go down it gets skinnier? That is a normal hail dent that can be repaired using PDR. When you feel the hail dent on a vehicle it feels like a cone getting skinnier and skinnier as it gets deeper. A hail dent that cannot be repaired by PDR has a floor. When you feel the hail dent, it has a cone shape and then hits a floor that is flat at the bottom of a dent.

This is a sign that the metal couldn't stretched any deeper and had to start stretching out at the bottom of the dent. This is called a cavern dent. Just like caverns have floors at the bottom, so do these types of dents. Caverns are either unable to be repaired or extremely difficult to be repaired with PDR.

Cracked Paint

When a hail stone hits on the edge of a panel, it can cause the paint to crack. The metal and paint cannot stretch past the edge of the panel, and therefore the paint gives and cracks. Cracked paint dents cannot usually be repaired with PDR.

The panel needs to now be painted and can no longer be "paintless dent repair". It is usually the right decision to write for a conventional repair when cracked paint is present. This can either be repair hours or a replacement of a panel. There are certain circumstances where a combination of PDR and conventional repair is the right choice, but that is beyond the scope of this chapter and book.

If you want more help with hail damage, I recommend grabbing my book called, Hail Adjuster's Playbook. It will guide you through how to get catastrophic hail deployments and claims and how to inspect and write them like a pro. I go into much further detail about the nuances or writing hail damage in that book.

Tire, Rim, and Suspension Damage

If you haven't realized it, most auto damage appraisers or adjusters are NOT mechanics (especially me!), and this is never more obvious than when I'm faced with damage to a vehicle's suspension parts.

The little guy in the picture above is me... except I never wear a tie, but the question marks are SPOT ON!

I have to give a shout out to my good friend Jody Roberts for his help with this chapter, particularly in the area of the suspension damage.

I'm going to break down what to do when faced with tire, rim, and suspension damage, and I will try my best to give you a no-nonsense guide to writing an intelligent estimate, even if you are like me and can't identify all the parts hidden behind the wheel.

I am going to assume that if you can identify all the parts or see additional damage that we DO NOT LIST that you will write it. I am trying to help you have a bare minimum list of what to write when faced with the following scenarios, but as always, your adjuster hat is on YOUR HEAD, not mine. You are the adjuster/appraiser, so you are responsible for what you write and for making the decision.

Tire Damage

- Replace Tire – Get Price (brand & size in notes)
- Mount and Balance Tire - $15

If a tire has a cut, gouge, is off the rim, etc. due to the loss, we will count that as tire damage.

 TIP **There is no "repairing" a tire. We REPLACE tires.**

Since we now know that we only replace tires, our job is straightforward. We must replace the tire, but what do we need to do?

First off, great a good photo of the damage. I've had companies not want to cover the tire because my picture wasn't good enough… that ends up in a supplement, get a good picture of the damage.

TIP **To get a good picture of the damage, you may need to push on the tire or take a different angle**

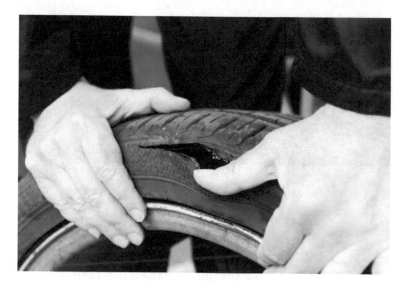

Also, get a good picture of the tire brand, type, and size. You may need to take two photos to get the size plus the brand name and type. The tire size numbers will be something like. 265/75R16 (see the picture below).

 If you can't read the tire brand or size on the damaged tire take a picture of the tire size on one of the UNDAMAGED tires (you are welcome in advance).

Lastly, we just need to get a part price for that tire. If your estimating software is set up to get the tire pricing, head to the tire section and put in the brand and size to locate the price.

If your estimating system doesn't have tire prices or doesn't include that tire price, head to Google and type in the brand and tire size to get a quick tire price from the great wide Internet.

At the time of this writing TireRack.com is an accepted site, but JUST MAKE SURE you get pricing for the correct size.

Google doesn't always show you what you typed in on the products section. In my example image, only ONE is the correct tire size.

Rim Damage

- Replace Rim - OEM or Recon $189 Keystone (check guidelines)
- 4-Wheel Alignment - $89.00
- Mount and Balance - $15
- Note - Possible additional damage that may become evident after alignment

When a rim is damaged, we want to replace the rim. Typically, if the vehicle qualifies for alternative parts, most guidelines indicate that you are able to use reconditioned rim or wheels.

Get a good picture of the rim to document the extent of the damage, and if possible, back up and take a photo showing WHICH rim it is. Insurance companies want perspective and like seeing it in relationship to the rest of the damage.

The most common vendor is Keystone, and I don't recommend you use anything else unless guidelines indicate. A reconditioned rim price is usually in your estimating system, if not $189 is the standard price.

If your estimating system doesn't have a part price built in, use a Reconditioned Rim $189 and input Keystone in the line notes as the vendor.

Suspension Damage

The suspension is often the most difficult to determine exactly what is damaged in the field inspection. Body shops and repair facilities often have to measure the suspension parts to determine if there is something damaged, and often in the field, we have a tire and rim blocking our view.

Suspension items, if damaged, must be replaced, and you'll need to check your guidelines to see if you are required/able to use aftermarket or recon parts on the suspension.

Don't use LKQ or used suspension parts.

Below are a suspension parts diagram, and I highly recommend, that if possible, you identify any parts that are damaged visually and take a photo of it.

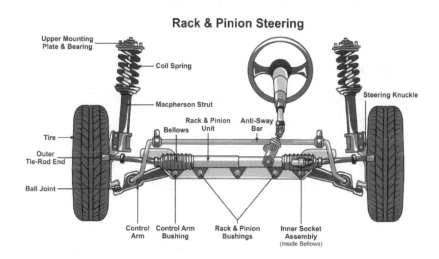

If you suspect suspension damage is possible, but can't visually confirm it, snap a few photos of the suspension by sticking your arm behind the tire to try and see what might be going on, and also to show you at least tried.

If you deem there is damage, but you can't see the individual components, I've included below what is normally damaged when a tire/rim has shifted in one direction or another. **Use at your discretion.**

 If you can't verify movement in the tire/rim indicating suspension damage or see any visual signs of damage to the suspension parts, put "Check Suspension" 1hr on the estimate.

Wheel Tilted In at Top or Bottom

- Replace Strut or Upper Control arm
- Replace Knuckle
- Replace Hub Bearing
- 4-Wheel Alignment - $89.00 (Unless a truck, then 2-wheel alignment $69, if only a front rim is damaged)
- Mount and Balance - $15
- Note – Possible additional damage that may become evident after alignment

See the image above for reference, but if the tire and rim were impacted and tilted back in towards the vehicle, either at the top or bottom, the strut or upper control arm is bent. The knuckle needs to be inspected for any stress. This is often visible from flaking. I would also figure a hub bearing due to it taking the force of the collision.

Check the strut tower or upper control arm mounts on the frame and look at the steering linkage any time a wheel has been damaged. The outer tie rod is the most common damaged component.

Wheel Shifted Forward or Backward

- Replace Strut or Upper Control Arm
- Replace Lower Control Arm
- Replace Knuckle
- Replace Hub Bearing

- 4-Wheel Alignment - $89.00 (Unless a truck, then 2-wheel alignment $69, if only a front rim is damaged)
- Mount and Balance - $15
- Note - Possible additional damage that may become evident after alignment

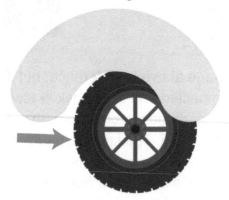

If the wheel is forward or backward, it is likely that the strut or upper control arm, lower control arm, knuckle, and bearings are all damaged.

Also, check the control arm mounting locations and strut tower. Inspect cradle for damage or movement (look at bolts to see if cradle has shifted) and look at the steering linkage any time a wheel has been damaged. The outer tie rod is the most common damaged component.

Part 3: The Playbook: Total Loss

Total Loss Process

This is one of the most confusing things about being an IA, understanding what a total loss is and how to handle the process.

The total loss definition on Wikipedia says it pretty straightforward,

> *"In insurance claims, a total loss is a situation where the lost value, repair cost or salvage cost of a damaged property exceeds its insured value. Such a loss may be an 'actual total loss' or a 'constructive total loss'."*

My version would go something like this,

"A total loss is where it doesn't make sense for the insurance company to fix the vehicle due to cost, safety, or legal reasons, and they pay out the value for the vehicle instead of repairing it."

How Do We Know a Vehicle is a Total Loss?

This is a question that most of my auto damage students are plagued with as they lay down at night. For the most part though, it isn't that difficult, and it gets easier with experience.

Most states have laws that insurance companies must abide by when it comes to damaged vehicles. As an example, some states require a vehicle to be "total lossed" if the damage to the vehicle exceeds 75% of the value of the vehicle.

Meaning?!?!?

If a vehicle is worth $10,000 and there is more than $7500 worth of damage, the insurance company is LEGALLY required to pay the full value for the vehicle ($10,000 in this case), minus the owner's deductible, if applicable.

We can know if a vehicle is a total loss through a few various methods.

1. **Estimating Software** - Audatex and CCC One have estimates of the percentage of a vehicles value based on your estimate (typically found in the upper right-hand corner of the estimate/damage screen).

2. **NADA Guide** – We can retrieve a NADA Guide/Value from NADAGuides.com and determine what 75% of the value of the vehicle will be.

3. **Valuation Companies** – There are vehicle valuation companies, such as CCC Value Scope and AutoSource, that run a real-time market analysis to determine the vehicles current value.

No matter how you determine the current value of the vehicle, or how close you are to a total loss, I have a quick tip for you.

 If a vehicle has sustained damage over 50% of its value on the initial inspection. I'd recommend a total loss in most scenarios. When in doubt... throw it out!

Total Loss Requirements

Most IA Firms and insurance companies have a new set of forms, photos, and requirements that you will need to satisfy once you determine a vehicle MAY be a total loss. The following chapters will help you walk through the different tasks you may encounter that I list here.

1. **Additional Photos** – Tread depth, interior, engine, fluids, etc.
2. **UPD Estimate** – Unrelated prior damage estimate
3. **Total Loss Valuation Form & Conditioning** – CCC, AutoSource, Mitchell, etc. documenting the options and condition of the vehicle
4. **NADA Guides** – PDF print off of the NADA value summary
5. **3 Comparables** – 3 similar vehicles that are for sale online.
6. **Salvage Bids** – Bids from Copart, IAA, Manheim or local salvage yards who will purchase the vehicle and sell as parts or at an auction.

If you need help with any of the tasks listed above, find the corresponding chapter. If you encounter a guideline not listed here, feel free to reach out to our community at www.IAPath.community

Unrelated (UPD) and Related Prior Damage

Few topics are as exciting, controversial, and full of cans of worms as this, prior damage.

Owners get upset when prior damage is written up, and insurance companies get frustrated when they pay for damages that are obviously not related to the loss they are covering.

There are two types of prior damage and understanding the differences between them is important. These two types of damages are:

1. Unrelated Prior Damage (UPD)
2. Related Prior Damage (RPD)

Unrelated Prior Damage

Unrelated prior damage, referred to here forward as UPD, is damage that existed before the damages/loss you are inspecting for and is in NO WAY related to that loss.

Basically, because the insurance company is responsible to pay the full value of a vehicle when it is total lossed, you are frequently asked to document UPD when a vehicle is a total loss.

For example, previous damage to the back door LOWERS the value of the vehicle, and the insurance company needs that documented to not be liable to pay for a vehicles full value is such damage exists. UPD tends to affect the VALUE of the vehicle.

Related Prior Damage

On the contrary, related prior damage, AKA RPD, tends to affect the repair amount. This damage is prior damage that DOES affect the repair we are writing up in addition to lowering the value of the vehicle.

If that same rear door damage exists and is, in fact, the same door that we are writing an estimate on (e.g. for someone backing up into the door), the insurance company is not required to fix the damage that existed on the door prior to the loss.

Even though it is "related", as in on the same panel, it was PRIOR. This will lower the number of repairs the insurance company is liable to pay because they don't have to fix that prior dent.

Documenting UPD or RPD

When you are required to write UPD or RPD, you document it in the estimating system differently, depending on which system you are using. Because this is such a common pain point for both the IA's and IA Firms, I want to instruct you how to document it in both estimating systems here.

UPD or RPD in CCC One

When writing your estimate in CCC One, you'll see a drop-down menu in the upper right-hand corner that indicates the type of estimate you are working on.

By default, this is set to "Estimate of Record". To document UPD or RPD, select the corresponding estimate type from the drop-down menu, as shown in the image below.

Once you select the UPD or RPD, any damages you have written will disappear! Don't fear, you can return to it by clicking the "Estimate of Record".

Any damages you write under the Unrelated Prior Damage or Related Prior Damage will be documented as a separate estimate. Be sure to print them off when you print your Estimate of Record.

UPD or RPD in Audatex

There are two ways to add unrelated prior damage (AKA UPD), and both happen inside of the "**Damage**" screen.

Ok, so you first must document the damage the same way you write damage on your estimate. Then, two ways you can add UPD is:

1. By clicking the "**UP**" box in the estimate line

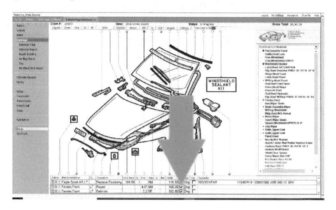

2. By clicking the "**UP**" box in the part edit window.

The unrelated prior damage estimate is printed automatically with the Estimate.

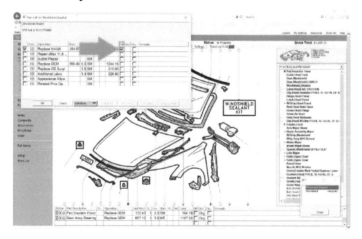

Make sure if that operation automatically added a refinish operation that you turned into UPD also marks the refinish as "UP".

Total Loss Forms

These forms are turned into the valuation companies or read off to them so they can run a market valuation on the vehicle. It can be time-consuming, up to fifteen minutes per form, even for a veteran to fill out.

It was always one of my least favorite tasks to do, and that is why I developed a software that fills out these forms for you in seconds. You can check it out at Autoforms.co (yes, that is .co not .com) if you are interested.

The forms contain the vehicle's options, mileage, and condition to allow for an accurate valuation based on the vehicle being total lossed.

I'll go through each section of the two major forms, CCC & AutoSource, but no matter which forms you fill out the information is the same.

CCC & AutoSource Valuation Forms

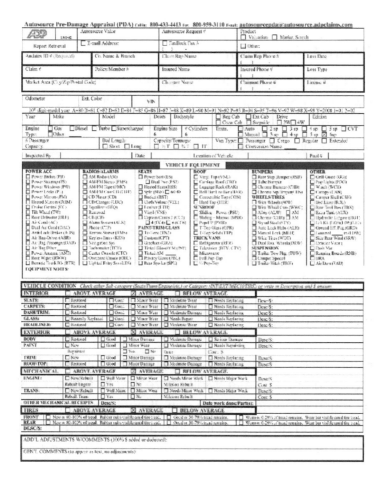

Both of these forms can be broken into three major sections.

1. Claim Information
2. Vehicle Information
3. Condition Information

Claim Information

This part of the form includes the claim number, owner's information, deductible, etc. All of this information can usually be found on your assignment sheet or on your estimate.

The Vehicle Information

The second part of the form lists all of the vehicle specific information, including: VIN, mileage, engine, options, etc. You can use your estimate, photos, software, or even the vehicle itself to determine all of this information.

Each option on the vehicle may represent a value increase or decrease. Make sure you fill this out with as much accuracy as you can. If anything is missing, or added in error, you are potentially stealing money from the insured or from the insurance company.

 Fill out the admin info and options for the vehicle on a total loss form in seconds using Autoforms.co

Condition Information

This is the final section of the form, where we rate the different parts of the vehicle based on its condition.

There are four ratings with the bottom representing the least good condition. The higher the rating, the better the condition.

This rating impacts the value of the vehicle HEAVILY. There are guidelines of how to rate each section accordingly, but I'll do my best to summarize here.

Fair – Bad condition, faded paint, ripped seats, etc.
Average - Standard vehicle condition, nothing special good or bad about it. Very typical.
Dealer – This is if something is perfectly restored or rarely been used. Use this sparingly.
Exceptional – No vehicle will ever be rated exceptional by an IA…. NEVER

 When rating a vehicle ALWAYS start rating everything as "Average" and let the vehicle convince you to rate it worse or better. If you deviate from "Average" you MUST add a note explaining why.

Calling in a Total Loss

Although uncomfortable, and never fun to call and talk to a valuation company, it really is a straightforward process.

1. Call the hotline number provided.

2. Follow the prompts to create a "New Valuation".

3. Enter the "office ID" informing them what insurance company it is for.

4. Give them the information from your filled-out form as they ask for it.

5. Write down the value and request/reference # they give you at the end.

6. Document both of the above numbers in your appraisal report.

 When giving a long number, such as a VIN or Claim # over the phone, use the phonetic chart below instead of saying individual letters. EXAMPLE: Instead of saying A, say "alpha". Say 123alpha instead of 123A.

A	Alpha
B	Bravo
C	Charlie
D	Delta
E	Echo
F	Foxtrot
G	Golf
H	Hotel
I	India
J	Juliet
K	Kilo
L	Lima

M	Mike
N	November
O	Oscar
P	Papa
Q	Quebec
R	Romeo
S	Sierra
T	Tango
U	Uniform
V	Victor
W	Whiskey
X	X-Ray
Y	Yankee
Z	Zulu

Vehicle Options Definitions

There are option definitions that explain EXACTLY how to determine if the vehicle you are inspecting has an option.

It is too lengthy to be included in this book, but you can access a downloadable guide of the options definitions for both CCC One and Audatex at AutoAdjustersPlaybook.com/guides

Nada Value & Guide

There will be claims that you are requested to get a NADA value on the vehicle you have inspected.

This can be due to it being a total loss or simply because they want to record what the vehicle is worth in case questions arise later. Reasons aside, getting a NADA Value is a straightforward process that doesn't take long.

Step 1: Head to NADAGuides.com

Once you arrive at the website, you'll be looking to get used car prices. At the time of this writing, the button is an obvious orange button that says, "Start Now".

Step 2: Choose the Vehicle

The next screen will allow you to choose the vehicle, by manufacturer or body style. I recommend you click the "Choose a Manufacturer" button.

For this example, we will be using a 2014 Honda Odyssey.

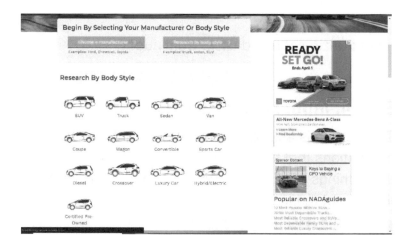

You'll need to locate your manufacturer (in this case Honda), the year, and model you are looking for from the list provided.

Once you've clicked on the model you are trying to get a value for, you'll now have to select the edition. Is it an EX, LE, LT, etc.

Choose the correct edition, and if you need help, reference the estimate you have written or the estimating software for those specifics. You can also check for badging in your photos if you are unsure.

Step 3: Enter the Zip Code

Upon choosing your editing, you'll have to input the zip code where the vehicle is located. This gives a value for the vehicle IN THAT zip code vs. just an annual average.

Input the zip code and click "Continue".

Step 4: Input Mileage and Options

This screen is asking for the mileage of the vehicle and options that the vehicle is equipped with. Both of these things affect the value of the vehicle. Take the time to get these things right.

If you need help with the options of the vehicle, double check your estimate and/or estimating software. These options are listed beneath the vehicle information, on the estimate or inside the options tab of your estimating software. Also, confirm all options using your photos when possible.

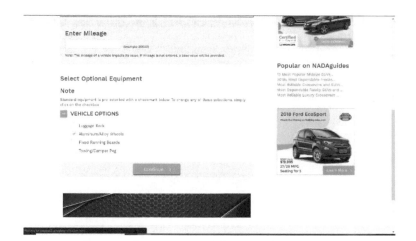

Step 5: Print the NADA Guide

Once the page finishes loading, you'll be able to see the "NADA Guide" with the different values of the vehicle.

To print off a copy for the IA Firm or insurance company, you'll need to click the "Print Friendly Button" so all the ads on the NADA website don't print off (see image below).

When the print-friendly version appears, you'll need to Right Click with your mouse on the screen and select "Print". This will print up your printer options.

Now, select the correct one to create a PDF and click "Print".

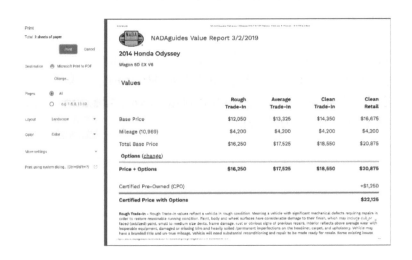

Save the file in your folder for this claim and upload it
to the company you are providing this for, and you are
DONE!

Getting 3 Comparable, Retail, or Auto Trader Ads

Certain total loss guidelines state that you need to obtain 3 comparables, 3 retail ads, or some even say Auto Trader Ads.

What they are looking for is vehicles that are close to the vehicle you are completing the total loss process on. This helps the insurance company establish what the vehicle is worth in the "real world".

The word comparable doesn't fully explain all the assumptions that come with it, so I decided to write an entire chapter on what an insurance company or IA Firm is looking for when they ask this and how to do it.

What Does Comparable Mean?

When you go and search for a comparable vehicle, you'll be looking for a vehicle that is similar in the following ways:

- Year
- Make
- Model
- Edition
- Mileage
- Condition
- Options
- Color (if possible)

It isn't always as easy as it sounds when searching for AutoTrader.com and similar sites.

The end goal is simple, obtain three comparable examples of the vehicle you are completing a total loss on, print the ads off as a PDF file, and write in your appraisal report the dollar amounts of each and the average of all three.

Some companies may have a separate form for you to fill out, so check your guidelines.

3 Comparable Example

The vehicle I inspected, and total lossed is a white 2015 Toyota Camry XLE with a V6. It has 77,147

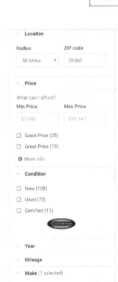

miles on it and is decked out with leather and all the bells and whistles.

Now head to AutoTrader.com (or similar site).

Type in your vehicle make, model and zip code.
On the left-hand side of the next screen, you'll see additional options you can adjust to dial in your search even further.

You'll want to input your year, check "used", and a mileage range. Go one mileage range above where the mileage of the vehicle is.

For my vehicle example it has 77,000, so I select "Under 100,000" miles.

I also checked the 6-cylinder box under the engine and added XLE as a keyword to help bring back only results that match the vehicle I'm looking for.

Once you've adjusted the options on the left, scroll down and click the magnifying glass/submit button.

This will re-submit your search based on your new criteria. Now, I'm going to sort the results by, "Mileage – Highest". The "sort by" button is in the upper left-hand corner.

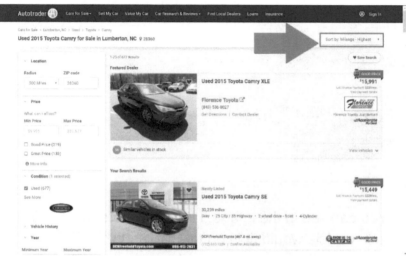

Scroll through your results looking for the vehicles that are closest in mileage and are the same "edition" as your vehicle. For my example, it is an XLE with 77,000 miles.

 **AutoTrader.com and similar sites typically have vehicles that are being "promoted" and/or "featured". This means they aren't all sorted in the correct mileage order as we requested. Make sure you scroll all the way**

through the promoted vehicles and get to the regular listings.

You can see in the image, I located where my 77,000 mile vehicle would fit in on this list, and I'm going to verify that the options are similar and print off the entire ad as a PDF. These are my three comparables because they are the same make, model, year, edition, engine, AND have similar mileage and options.

To print, click into each ad, right-click the screen and select your PDF printer to save it digitally.

Salvage Bids

It isn't fun to get Salvage bids for a client. The insurance company has you get salvage bids so they know what they can get as salvage/scrap for the vehicle.

Companies, like IAA and Copart, pick apart salvage yards and will pay money for total lossed vehicles. They, in turn, re-sell it either as a whole or in parts.

The price the salvage yard pays for the vehicle lowers the insurance company's cost when they must total loss a vehicle.

The major yards are quick and easy to deal with. But, finding a local place to give a "bid" or quote is tough. I'd avoid the word bid and use "quote", or just ask if they buy totaled vehicles...or they might not understand what you're asking. Local places don't really like giving these quotes, and if they do ---they're very low.

When asked to get 3 salvage bids, here are my suggestions:

1. Find a local salvage yard (or semi-local) that will give you salvage "quotes" (they won't always give bids, but may give a courtesy quote even if its $100 and they don't want the car... THAT COUNTS!) SAVE THIS # and company. Use them for a quick quote.

2. Call Copart and get a pro quote. (They'll ask a few details and get you a price) Call 800-381-6219 select Pro Quote. Then you will be directed to someone to give the vehicle information to. It's much like call in to CCC, just not as in depth. They will give you a value on the vehicle

3. Call IAA (Independent Auto Auction) and get a quote from them.

Part 3: The Playbook: Supplement

Completing a Supplement

A supplement is an additional payment that is required to cover the entire cost of a vehicle's repairs.

The facility that is repairing the vehicle will submit a supplement request if they find additional damages, additional operations, or part price changes that cause an INCREASE in the final bill.

Now it is our job to determine if the supplement is legitimate, to add the additional items to our original estimate that we created, if need be, re-inspect the vehicle, and upload it to the IA Firm or insurance carrier we are working under for that claim.

4 Steps to a Completed Supplement

5. Review the Supplement
6. Re-inspect the Supplement
7. Match the Supplement

8. Upload the Supplement

Ok, when we left the vehicle last, it was at the owner's residence, damaged. We uploaded the estimate to the appraisal and insurance company and moved on with our lives, looking forward to getting paid for the inspection.

Well, the life of that claim and the owner goes on as well. The owner will want to get the vehicle repaired at a shop of their choice, and whenever the vehicle makes its way into the shop, there will likely be something you missed or couldn't see during the original inspection.

The shop will complete a teardown of the vehicle. A teardown is the process of removing all the parts that are hindering the shop from seeing all the damage the vehicle has. Once the shop completes a teardown of the vehicle, their estimator will go over the damages and will put together a supplement.

A supplement is a revised estimate with additional or supplement items that were originally missed. The shop will then email or fax over their supplement to the insurance or appraisal company. Once they receive the supplement, they will notify you that you have a supplement for your file. It is possible that the shop submit the supplement directly to you, if they do, notify the IA Firm and they will open up the claim for a supplement.

In many ways this process can feel difficult. You rarely are ever paid for a supplement, and the estimate now must be an agreed price with a shop, but rest easy, it isn't that hard.

Let's go over the 4 Steps to a Complete Supplement.

Step 1: Review the Supplement

The great news is the burden is on the shop to prove to you that they need additional parts, labor, and operations. You can ask a lot of questions before the shop feels like you are clueless! If you don't understand why a shop is asking for an item or operation, you can simply ask. That's getting ahead of myself. I just wanted to put your mind at ease.

When you receive, the supplement, download it. It's usually uploaded into the appraisal management system where you uploaded the photos and original estimate. Look to see if the shop sent over any photos or other documents. If any additional documents were included download all images and documents provided.

Open the supplement PDF document and look at the estimate. On the left-hand side of the estimate will usually be an "S1", representing supplement 1, next to all items that were added or changed since your original estimate. This is your roadmap.

Review all the S1 items, review the shop photos if included, and your original photos and see if any items are confusing or you disagree with.

If it all makes perfect sense and the supplemental dollar amount is under $1500, you may not have to re-inspect this vehicle. If it's a large supplement or there are questionable items, you may need to visit the shop within the next 48 hours and re-inspect the vehicle.

If it's a $1500 and under supplement, but no photos were included, call the shop completing the repairs and ask for images and/or invoices to be sent over to support the request for additional items requested.

Review the images and make sure you don't have any questions.

Step 2: Re-inspect the Supplement

If you must re-inspect the vehicle, due to the size of the supplement or items that you disagree with, call the shop and verify the vehicle is on site and ask to speak to the estimator who is handling the file.

Once you arrive, visit the front desk and inform them that you are there to re-inspect Mr. Smith's vehicle and spoke with Matt, their estimator. The shop will ask if you need a copy of the supplement, SAY YES!

When the estimator takes you to the vehicle go through the supplement, line by line, with them there, taking photos of each item on the supplement.

If everything makes sense there on site with the shop, get your photos and let them know you will upload the supplement to the insurance company.

If you and the shop can't come to an agreement, you may need to call your inside adjuster or the appraisal company you are working for, and ask for their guidance, but always try and resolve it between you and the shop.

No matter how you got to this point of the supplement, you now have an agreed repair in a supplement sheet and photos that support those items. GREAT!

Step 3: Match the Supplement

With your agreed repair, go back to your estimating system and open the original estimate that you created for this vehicle. Go to the damages screen (in CCC One) and click "Create a Supplement".

Take the shop supplement and go to the bottom of the supplement. Find the Supplement Summary. This is a list of only the items that were changed, deleted, or added. Make the changes in your estimating software to match the supplement from the shop.

If you can't figure out where a part of the vehicle is located, simply scroll up to the supplement of record where it shows the part groupings on the supplement, and find the part or operation under that grouping.

Once you have completed all the lines of the supplement into your estimating system, review the total dollar amounts and make sure your estimate is the same or close to the shop's final amount.

If there is a large difference, review the labor rates, taxes, and labor hours on the totals page of the supplement versus your supplement in CCC One.

When times get real tough, walk away from the computer then come back to review and go over it again. You need this supplement to be close if not exact!

This will be the amount that the insurance company pays out for the supplement, and the shop will fight for this money if it is far off. In the event you can't match it, email it to the shop and ask them if they will review it and see if you missed anything. They will usually find the items you missed quickly and tell you the difference.

Step 4: Upload the Supplement

Once you feel comfortable with how close your supplement matches the shops, you now go through the process of uploading the supplement, photos, and appraisal report, just like you did your original estimate into the appraisal system.

6. Lock the supplement
7. Print out a copy of the PDF
8. Upload the PDF and photos to the appraisal system
9. Write a Supplement 1 appraisal report
10. Close the file

You've now handled the supplement! Make sure you understand the repairs enough so that if you get a call from the adjuster you can answer their questions. If you don't know the answer to an adjuster's question(s), let them know you will review the file to remind yourself and call them back with the answer.

Review the file, talk to the shop to verify why an operation was needed (if need be) and call back the adjuster with an answer.

Next Steps

WOW! You made it through the book, congratulations! I hope you've found and continue to find this book informative and a useful as a quick reference guide for years to come.

I wrote this book based on what I teach my high end coaching and mentoring students who become my auto apprentice through the program I call the Auto Adjuster's Path.

If you are interested in having a mentor or learning more about being an auto IA and how to get work as an auto IA head over to IAPath.com/auto.

We provide all the training, mentorship, support, and relationships with IA Firms so you can get work FAST!

If you need someone to call, celebrate a victory with, talk about a problem, or just so you know that you aren't alone, I encourage you to reach out to me. The quickest way to get me is by sending an email to Chris@IAPath.com or you can connect to me on LinkedIn at www.Linkedin.com/IAPath.

If you'd rather talk on the phone, you can choose a time from my calendar at www.calendly.com/iapath.

For additional information about being or becoming an IA, there are 140+ episodes (at the time of this writing) on my Independent Adjuster's Podcast. This weekly audio show will give you inspiration and information on the go absolutely free. You can find all the episodes at www.IAPath.com/podcast, and of course, on iTunes, Google, Stitcher, or whatever podcast app you listen to.

I'm honored that you have spent this much time with me, and I pray daily that the work I do helps people just like you. You are what makes IA Path so amazing, and this industry needs you. They don't need another licensed adjuster, they NEED YOU! Someone that is passionate enough to read through a book on the topic. Someone invested enough to want to know how to do it right. We in this industry desperately need genuine people who care. If I can ever help you succeed in this journey, don't hesitate to reach out. Remember, that is why I am here.

Keep walking your path and *Claim Your Life*!

Your Guide,
Chris Stanley

URGENT PLEA!

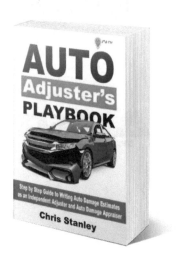

THANK YOU FOR READING MY BOOK!

I appreciate any feedback, and I love hearing what you have to say. I need your input to make the next version of this book and my future books better.

Please leave me a helpful review on Amazon letting me (and others) know what you thought of the Auto Adjuster's Playbook.

Thank you so much!!

Chris Stanley

Independent Adjuster Paths
by IA Path

If you want an all in one solution along with online mentorship and training, jump into the Path of your choice by going to my website

Head to IAPath.com